American
HOME COOKING

American
HOME COOKING
Favourite recipes from all over the USA

KENNA LACH BIFANI · MIRANDA WHYTE

Macdonald Orbis

A *Macdonald Orbis* BOOK

© Macdonald & Co., 1987

Published in Great Britain in 1987
by Macdonald & Co (Publishers) Ltd
London & Sydney

A member of BPCC plc

British Library Cataloguing in Publication Data
Whyte, Miranda
  American home cooking.
  1. Cookery, American
  I. Title   II. Bifani, Kenna Lach
  641.5973   TX715

ISBN 0-356-15087-9

Filmset by SX Composing Ltd

Printed and bound in Italy by Graphicom

Senior editor: Judith More
Text editor: Judy Martin
Art director: Roberta Colgate Stone
Designer: Frances de Rees
Photographer: Jerry Tubby
Stylist: Sarah Wiley
Home Economists: Jill Eggleton, Joyce
Harrison

Macdonald & Co (Publishers) Ltd
Greater London House
Hampstead Road
London   NW1 7QX

Contents

INTRODUCTION

'*As* *with just about everything, this book was born of the union of two impulses. The first was the intense frustration I felt when faced with American recipes which called for ingredients I had never heard of, requiring them to be measured in, of all things, cups! Breakfast cups? Coffee cups? Or didn't it matter? – I hadn't a clue! In desperation, I turned to my American friend, Kenna, who patiently explained that a cup was a specific measure and showed me how it was possible to measure a quarter cup of butter!*

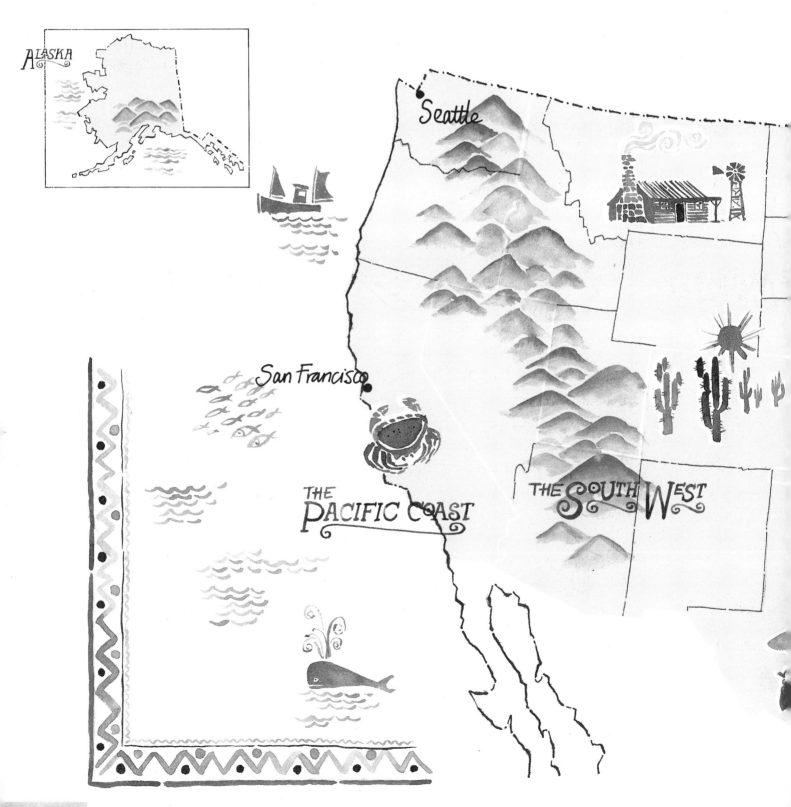

The book's other raison d'être was Kenna's desire to prove that American food is not all 'fast food' of the type they export the world over, but is rich in variety, exciting in tastes, and drawn from a great many other cuisines – as polyglot as America itself! On page 8 Kenna explains what, to her, American food really means, and in the introduction to each collection of recipes gives you the background to each region of the US and its food.

We have translated the recipes into 'English', using substitutes for some American

ingredients which are unavailable here. There is a difference in terminology, which makes some of the recipe titles strike the English ear a little oddly, when you look at the ingredients and method. 'Barbecued', for example, means a particular cooking method to us, whereas in the States it tends to refer to something cooked or marinaded in a barbecue sauce – slightly spicy and tomato-based. The famous Sloppy Joes are also known as Barbecued burgers – even more confusing as they are not actually burgers, having a 'sloppy' consistency – but they are made with minced beef, hence the title 'burger'. In addition, you will notice that some of the Southern recipes call for catfish: this is not the same as the fish sold here under that name, so don't try it even if you can find it. We have substituted huss, which works out just as well. Other differences are explained in the listing of terms on page 172.

All measurements have been converted into metric and imperial measures, so you won't have to master the US cup system. But because we hope this book will excite both your taste buds and your interest enough to set you hunting hungrily for more, we also provide a brief table of the most commonly used ingredients, giving their metric and imperial weights equivalent to the US cup, and a table of liquid measures (see page 173). Teaspoons and tablespoons are roughly equivalent between the US and metric measures, and we have ignored the tiny difference if you are still using imperial measuring spoons – you have our word there is not one recipe in which this will matter either way.

Many of these recipes are firm favourites with Kenna's family and friends, and as she is now living in England, though much travelled, it hasn't been difficult to ensure that you will be able to find all the less familiar ingredients in your local supermarket. For a few others, we've had a great time trying out equivalents and substitutes, mixing and matching until the tastes and textures seem exactly right. For those of you coming to American cooking for the first time, I hope you'll be as amazed and delighted as I have been by its variety and inventiveness. Read on, and enjoy! '

'*M*ost people, when asked the question, 'What is American food?' will think of fast foods, such as those served at burger bars, or the prepackaged 'just add water, set for five minutes and there's your meal' variety sold at supermarkets. If they've eaten at 'American-style' restaurants, they may even add Barbecue ribs or Chicago-style deep-pan pizza to the list. If really pushed, they may possibly mention Blueberry pie, Boston baked beans, Brownies, and perhaps Clam chowder or Hash, Pumpkin pie and Waffles. These are legacies of Hollywood films of the fifties – food they've heard tell of but never eaten. Many Americans who have lived only in one section of the country and never travelled, or those who are sixteen years old and want to be part of the gang, may well say the same thing!

I have lived for several years each in the Midwest, the Deep South, the Bayou country, the Pacific Coast, and the Southwest, feasting on the local fare, and collecting recipes everywhere I went. So, in the following pages, you will find recipes for Hamburgers and Southern fried chicken, for Pizza, for Chowder and Hash, Pumpkin pie and Brownies too, but you will also discover the wonders of spicy Creole cooking, the exotic Polynesian delights of Hawaiian food, the home-cooking comforts of Midwestern meals, the fire of Tex-mex, and much, much more.

The USA was originally settled by the outcasts and rebels from many other countries, each group gravitating towards the area most like their homeland. Hence, those of German, Scandinavian and Slavic ancestry predominate in the Midwest, while the Mexicans settled in the Southwest. They brought their culture with them, adapting their cuisine to what was locally available, and adding new things learned from the natives (American Indians, Hawaiians). The staples of diet vary region by region, reflecting the natural abundance of indigenous foods, and what the settlers discovered could be best grown or raised there: for example, chicken and corn in the South, and fish and rice in the Bayou country.

Of course, over the years refrigeration, transportation, and communication have improved, thus making most things available in any area of the country. In addition, people move from one region to another with much more frequency than was the case fifty years ago, so there has been increased integration. I remember moving from Milwaukee to San Francisco twenty-five years ago and seeing artichokes and avocados for the first time: now they are found in supermarkets in every state.

We finish with a chapter called Across the Board, which includes recipes, perhaps of mixed or obscure origin, which are commonly eaten from coast to coast. Elsewhere recipes have been assigned to their region of origin, or to the region in which they are now most prevalent, although they, too, may be eaten in many or all areas of the country. In putting the book together, we have, in general, selected our favourite recipes from each region, so certainly the list is not all inclusive. Some very common recipes have been omitted because of extreme cost, or unavailability of an essential ingredient or acceptable substitute.

A word on eating habits since we're sure you've observed Americans eating with their forks upside down, placing their knives on the plate after cutting the meat. I've been told by an English friend that the habit originated because in the early settlement days there were not enough knives to go round. I wonder where the forks came from!

In general, I have found the style of eating, barring that in posh restaurants or in the homes of those of the higher social echelons, to be far more informal than in the UK, and, since the American workday begins early mealtimes are earlier too.

Another difference is in the type of foods eaten at particular meals: take breakfast. In a stateside coffee-house or restaurant, the variety of a breakfast menu is mind boggling. In addition to the ten different egg dishes, it includes perhaps twenty varieties of Pancakes, Waffles, Chipped beef on toast, just to name a few. Many are items more commonly seen on a dessert menu here. Oh, and don't be shocked when you see Yanks putting marmalade on the 'fried bread', and eating it with their eggs. Toast is normally eaten with the eggs rather than after, and they have no idea what 'fried bread' is – in America, it's dipped in egg, fried in butter, and called French toast! I must say though, that as mums and dads race off to work, and the children to school, the norm now, as it is here, is to grab a bowl of cereal or a piece of toast. Full-scale breakfasts are reserved for weekends and for business meetings.

Brunch is a meal that has become quite common as a Sunday social event, comparable to the British custom of going to the pub before returning home for the Sunday joint. Since American women refuse to allow the men to go off and enjoy a jar while they slave in the kitchen, brunches are more often eaten in restaurants than at home. They usually begin in the late morning and last over several hours. They are a more substantial meal than breakfast (even the American breakfast!) and often include champagne or other morning drinks like Bloody Mary. In New Orleans, jazz brunches are a well-known feature: the bands play, food is chosen from three or four tables laden with a variety of dishes, and you get a champagne refill each time you have a sip from the glass!

Though tea can be had, coffee is the preferred beverage, and it is consumed with or without a snack, at any time and usually throughout the day. Afternoon tea as a meal is unheard of, except as a passing fashion in some major cities; cakes are more usually eaten as desserts.

The evening meal, even when entertaining guests, is still a pretty informal affair. Most Americans will serve drinks and hors d'oeuvres in the living room, proceeding to the table only for soup and bread, or main course and salad. They will then return to the living room where, after dinner is digested, they will have coffee, dessert and a liqueur.

So now feel free to impress your American friends when they visit, but be prepared for their disappointment – I think, in most cases, they can hardly wait to try fish and chips, steak and kidney pie, and roast beef and Yorkshire pudding! For you who are used to these things, I hope American cooking proves a new and exciting area.

chapter

1.

The Bayou Country

Creole/Cajun
Cooking

*Y*ou may wonder why this region is only a small section *(the Gulf Coast, around New Orleans), while others are vast, often encompassing several states. The Bayou country, although a part of the Deep South, seems to be totally set apart from it, and from the rest of the country, by its people and its food, its habits, language and architecture and, too, its wonderful music. It was in this area that the French-speaking Acadians, expelled from Nova Scotia by the British in the 1700s, joined the Spaniards and the black slaves already settled there. This combination of ethnic groups created a unique culture, and the tastiest food which can be called American.*

We begin with this section because it is our favourite, and we are unlikely to be alone in saying that. In England, a conversation always includes a comment on the weather; in New Orleans, and its surrounding countryside, conversation always returns to food – its role in life is that important! One never tires of the various dishes, and for everyone who has lived there, wherever else they go, eating will never mean as much.

Rice is grown in this hot, humid, marshy environment, and seafood is plentiful; you will note that most of the starters and main dishes include these staples. There are a few basic ingredients commonly used: in the vegetable line, green peppers, spring onions, celery; seasonings include Tabasco sauce, cayenne pepper, bay leaves and thyme, salt and black pepper, with parsley and garlic. Most of the recipes are quite simple yet achieve mouthwateringly delicious effects. The food is spicy hot, so be prepared! You may, of course, use less cayenne and Tabasco, but don't then tell your friends you're serving them a real Creole or Cajun dish!

Traditionally, gumbo recipes use a herb called filé: it is made from dried sassafras leaves, and is unavailable here. As it is basically a thickening agent, we have substituted cornflour – the gumbo is still superb!

We mentioned rice being a mainstay of the Creole/Cajun diet. I learned to cook rice from a Cajun woman – the method's ever so easy and never fails. Pour water into a pan, and add salt. Put your finger in vertically and measure how far up your finger the water comes; then add an amount of rice that brings the water level up by the same depth again. Bring to the boil, with the lid on, turn down the heat and leave for twenty minutes. A Cajun can teach you more little tricks with food than you could learn in two years of cookery classes!

Shrimp remoulade

❝Cool, crunchy, tangy, spicy, juicy – a super starter for those who like food with a zing! It is best if the dish is prepared the day before use, as the marinade needs to rest, preferably overnight. ❞

Serves: 8.
1.5 kg/3 lb unshelled prawns
2-3 tbsp horseradish mustard
2 tbsp paprika
I tsp cayenne
4 tsp salt
about 150 ml/5 fl oz tarragon vinegar
about 350 ml/12 fl oz salad oil (not olive)
1-1½ bunches spring onions, coarsely chopped
2-3 medium celery sticks, finely chopped
4 tbsp fresh parsley, chopped
2-3 cloves garlic, crushed
I iceberg lettuce, shredded

1 In a large mixing bowl, stir together the horseradish mustard, paprika, cayenne and salt, beating well with a wire whisk.
2 Add the vinegar and then, beating constantly, add the oil, pouring in a thin stream. Continue to beat until the sauce is thick and smooth.
3 Add the onions, celery, parsley and garlic, mixing well.
4 Cover tightly with clingfilm and leave for several hours, or overnight.
5 At least two hours before you want to serve, add the prawns to the marinade.
6 To serve, make beds of shredded lettuce on individual serving dishes, and ladle prawns and some of the marinade on top.

Marinated crabs

❝A delicious starter, but quadruple the amounts and you have a pretty good party dip! Best made the day before since the longer it has to marinate, the better it tastes. ❞

Serves: 4.
450g/I lb crab meat
½ medium onion, finely chopped
I stick celery, finely chopped
¼ green pepper, finely chopped
Marinade:
600 ml/20 fl oz salad oil (not olive)
120 ml/4 fl oz white wine vinegar
I tsp Worcester sauce
1½ tsp Tabasco
I tsp salt
½ tsp black pepper
I bay leaf
pinch of thyme
pinch of allspice
some grated lemon peel
squeeze of lemon juice
For serving:
I lettuce
I lemon

1 Prepare the crab meat. If frozen, allow time to thaw, and squeeze out excess moisture.
2 Prepare the vegetables.
3 Mix all the ingredients of the marinade, add the crab meat and vegetables, and marinate for several hours, preferably overnight.
4 Serve on a bed of lettuce, and garnish with lemon wedges. Use a slotted spoon, or try to drain off some of the marinade; otherwise the lettuce swiftly reduces to a soggy mess, and the whole takes on the appearance of a floating island, which is not quite the desired effect!

Crab dip

Makes: about 600 ml/20 fl oz.
450 g/1 lb white crab meat
1 x 30 g/1¼ oz pkt French onion soup
600 ml/20 fl oz sour cream

1 If using frozen crab meat, allow to thaw, and then squeeze out all the excess moisture, or the dip will be too runny.
2 Blend the dry soup mix with the sour cream, and fold in the crab meat.
3 Chill well – at least 4-5 hours – and serve with wheat crackers.

Oysters rockefeller

❛Don't be put off if you've never tackled oysters – these are simple to prepare, the oysters are cooked and the whole thing is utterly delicious. This recipe also makes a lovely light lunch or super brunch dish, followed by warm croissants; or, you might serve it late, for a rather special supper of the *à deux* variety, with a bottle of bubbly . . .

Rock salt is recommended in the recipe, but if you can't get it, buy packets of the cheapest cooking salt available. You need a couple of shallow tins, in which you make a salt bed where you lay the oysters in the half-shell (deep half), while they cook. The salt bed holds them in position so they don't spill their contents. ❜

Serves: 4.
24 oysters
rock salt, enough to make at least 2.5 cm/1 in depth in baking tins
Sauce:
2-3 large bunches spring onions, very finely chopped
675 g/1½ lb fresh spinach, very finely chopped
2 bunches fresh parsley, very finely chopped
350 g/12 oz butter or margarine
6-8 cloves garlic, crushed
85 g/3 oz flour
up to 2 tbsp anchovy paste or sauce
1 tsp cayenne
1½ tsp salt
up to 4 tbsp Pernod, or other anise-based alcohol

1 Prepare the vegetables and keep them all in a bowl together, ready to add to the sauce later.
2 Make a level bed of salt in each of the two baking pans, and place in the oven at 180°/350°/Gas Mark 4, to warm through.
3 Shuck the oysters: do this over a bowl so you catch the juice. If you don't happen to have an oyster knife in your kitchen drawer, pick a good, strong but fairly short-bladed knife. We use a Swiss army penknife. Force the knife blade in between the shells near the hinge, and sever the muscle. Don't worry about pieces of grit or shell – the juice is strained later. Carefully remove the oysters to another bowl, and keep the deep half-shells, which should now be cleaned well, and dried.
4 Rinse the oysters gently in cold water and drain, reserving at least 600 ml/20 fl oz of this water. Gently dry the oysters on kitchen towels.
5 Strain the oyster juice through muslin or a coffee-filter paper, and reserve. The 24 oysters should yield about 300 ml/10 fl oz juice, to which you will need to add about 450 ml/15 fl oz of the reserved rinsing water. (Hang on to the rest – you may need it later to add to the sauce.)
6 Melt the butter/margarine in a large saucepan. Add the garlic, and brown gently. Then add the flour and blend well, stirring all the time.
7 Slowly add the oyster juice and rinsing water liquid. Stir well and cook until the sauce thickens. (Use more of the reserved liquid if necessary.)
8 Now add the seasoning – go easy with the anchovy paste, adding gradually, and tasting as you go; it can be very strong. Add the cayenne and salt, and mix well.
9 Add the vegetables, stirring in well, and simmer gently until they are soft (but don't overcook – time will depend on the size of the vegetable pieces).
10 Add the Pernod and let the sauce cook gently for a few minutes so the flavour develops.
11 Remove the salt pans from the oven. Lay each oyster in a shell and place gently on salt bed, pressing it into the salt carefully so it is firmly held in position. Add 2 tablespoons sauce to cover each oyster, taking care to keep it within the shell. Place the tins in the oven and cook for 15 minutes or so – the sauce should be bubbling and just browning. (If you prefer, you can finish them off under the grill.)
12 Place 6 oysters in their shells on each plate, and serve. Any remaining sauce can be served in a warmed dish or sauce boat.

Eggs hussarde

We served this for a summer Sunday brunch and our friends were most impressed! It is very rich, quite unusual and delicious, but it is also fiddly and quite time-consuming; something, we think, to be attempted only for special occasions. If you find sauces easy then you may find this a snip, but if you don't ...... there is the odd moment when you feel that octopoidal features would be advantageous. But its reception well repaid us!

Serves: 6.
6 eggs
300 ml/10 fl oz Marchand de Vin sauce (see recipe below)
300 ml/10 fl oz Hollandaise sauce (see recipe below)
6 slices green (unsmoked) bacon – back is good
1-2 large firm tomatoes (beef tomatoes are good for this)
3 'English-style' muffins, halved
butter or margarine for frying and poaching
paprika

1 If you are starting from scratch, make the Marchand de Vin and Hollandaise sauces.
2 Heat the oven, on low, and set serving plates to warm.
3 Grill the bacon well; cut tomatoes into 5 mm/¼ in slices; heat the sauces gently.
4 Halve the muffins, place one half on each plate and top with a slice of well-grilled bacon. Ladle on a spoonful of Marchand de Vin sauce, and replace in the oven to keep warm.
5 Fry the tomato slices, gently. Heat poaching water, then place the eggs to poach.
6 Place a tomato slice on top of each muffin, and keep warm. When the eggs are cooked, place an egg on each muffin, and ladle on to each about 2 tablespoons Hollandaise sauce. Sprinkle with a pinch of paprika and serve immediately.

Marchand de vin sauce

This is a very rich and fairly strong-tasting sauce. If you have any left over from a main recipe, try it over rice, or even on toast!

Makes: about 450 ml/15 fl oz.
4-5 spring onions, finely chopped
½ small onion, finely chopped
2-3 cloves garlic, crushed
4 small mushrooms, finely chopped
3 slices (about 85 g/3 oz) lean smoked ham, finely chopped
115 g/4 oz butter
25 g/1 oz flour
225 ml/8 fl oz chicken stock, or bouillon
120 ml/4 fl oz dry red wine
salt and pepper

1 Prepare and chop all vegetables, and the ham.
2 In a saucepan, melt the butter, add the onions and garlic, and cook until soft, but don't allow to brown. Add the mushrooms, and cook until soft. Add the flour, mixing well. Add ham pieces.
3 Now, stirring constantly with a wire whisk, gradually add the stock and then the wine.
4 Cook, stirring, until the sauce thickens. Add seasoning.

Hollandaise sauce

This sauce is very rich, and not easy to make. We both have nightmares about making Hollandaise, and if you aren't good at sauces, we heartily recommend using a packet mix. Purists might object, but for peace of mind and reduced stress when entertaining, go ahead!

Makes: about 600 ml/20 fl oz.
4 egg yolks
225-275 g/8-10 oz unsalted butter
1 tbsp cold water
2 tbsp lemon juice (strained) plus juice of ½ lemon
½ tsp salt and ¼ tsp white pepper

1 Cut the butter into small pieces and melt in a saucepan. Cover to keep warm.
2 Separate the eggs and put the egg yolks in the top pan of a double boiler. Add the cold water, and beat with a wire whisk until mixture is foamy.
3 Place the top pan into the double boiler – the water below must not be hot enough to allow the sauce to boil. Keeping the heat low, beat until the mixture thickens and doubles in volume. Do not boil. Pour in the melted butter slowly, but don't stop whisking until the sauce thickens.
4 Add the lemon juice and seasoning.

Left: Oysters rockefeller (recipe, page 13)

Eggs sardou

'This is a particularly good dish – less rich than Eggs hussarde, and altogether lighter. It is traditionally served in New Orleans as a brunch dish, but it would make a very tasty starter for a dinner, or a light brunch or supper dish. A simpler version is to mix the artichoke hearts, sliced, with the spinach sauce, and omit the Hollandaise. '

Serves: 6.
6 eggs
900 g/2 lb fresh spinach (when stripped, this reduces to about 550 g/1¼ lb)
300 ml/10 fl oz Hollandaise sauce (see recipe on page 15)
25 g/1 oz butter or margarine, and a little extra for frying and poaching
15 g/½ oz flour
300 ml/10 fl oz milk
½ tsp salt
dash of white pepper
6 artichoke hearts

1 Prepare the spinach: strip leaves from stalks, wash, and cook in very little water, until just soft. Drain well, squeeze out excess, and chop coarsely.
2 At this point make the Hollandaise sauce if you have none in store. Keep warm.
3 Melt 25 g/1 oz butter/margarine, stir in the flour, allow to cook a minute or two, and pour in the milk, stirring constantly with a wire whisk, until the sauce is thickened and smooth.
4 Stir in the spinach, and season with salt and pepper. Cover and set aside.
5 Melt a little butter in a frying pan or skillet. Add the artichoke hearts, topside down, and allow to heat through gently, basting with the butter. Sprinkle with a little salt, cover, and leave on a very low heat.
6 Meanwhile, poach the eggs gently.
7 When the eggs are ready, spoon the spinach mixture onto warmed serving plates, place an artichoke heart on each bed of spinach sauce, top with an egg, and spoon some Hollandaise sauce over the whole. Serve immediately.

Coush-coush (Fried cornmeal)

'However boring it may sound, this is a wonderful breakfast or brunch dish – a sort of Cajun version of porridge! When we served it, we were met with suspicious questions followed, on tasting, with sounds of delight and amazement – and the rush to the table to try it with different fruits and syrups! '

Serves: 4-6.
225 g/8 oz yellow cornmeal (polenta)
50 g/2 oz plain flour
1 tbsp baking powder
115 g/4 oz sugar
2 tbsp salt
350 ml/12 fl oz water
about 150 g/5 oz fat (we use margarine or half-and-half margarine and butter)

1 Combine the cornmeal, flour, baking powder, sugar and salt in a large mixing bowl. Add the water and mix to a smooth paste.
2 Melt 115 g/4 oz fat in the pan. (Use a 23 cm/9 in or 25 cm/10 in frying pan, or skillet – cast iron is best. At a later stage, you'll need a lid, or foil to cover.) Add the cornmeal mixture, patting it flat into the pan. Increase the heat and fry until brown and crusty on the bottom. Stir, distributing bits of the crust throughout.
3 Check consistency – you may like to add more fat if it looks too dry, or if you like a richer buttery taste. Add about another 25 g/1 oz.
4 Reduce heat, cover, and cook for further 10-15 minutes, stirring occasionally.
5 Spoon into bowls, and serve with syrup, stewed fruit, jams, or milk and sugar. It goes wonderfully well with Blueberry syrup – its sweet fruitiness is just right, and the dark purplish blue looks mouthwateringly wonderful on the buttery golden coush-coush. Golden syrup is fine too, but a sharper tang is more complementary. Try it with maple syrup, any sort of fruit syrup, or slightly melted jam – black cherry is delicious.

Chicken gumbo

This is tangy, tasty and very filling, and can best be described as a meal-in-itself soup (despite Kenna's protestations: 'It's a GUMBO!'). Well, it *is* a gumbo, and takes its place in the meal in much the way a hearty bowl of minestrone or pistou would; of course, you can serve it as a starter, too. It is relatively inexpensive to make, and although it requires diligence, it is well worth the effort. It can easily be made in advance – it does not lose its flavour, and is good for several days.

In the Bayou country, gumbo (which can also be made with prawns, pork, pigeon – and the Cajuns even cook robin gumbo) is traditionally a Sunday lunch family meal, but Kenna often ate it at local restaurants, late at night, after a party, an evening's drinking or a bowling session.

Serves: 4-6 as a main course. It would probably do 8-10 as a soup.
Brown roux:
115 g/4 oz plain flour
120 ml/4 fl oz vegetable oil (this is a generous measure)
Gumbo:
1 boiling chicken (cut into individual portions, so weight depends on how many
you are feeding)
5 dried hot red peppers
3 large bay leaves
1½ tsp crushed thyme
4 tsp salt
about 4.5-5.5 l/8-10 pts water
4 cloves garlic, crushed
1 onion, coarsely chopped
225 g/8 oz okra, cut into 2.5 cm/1 in pieces
1 green pepper, coarsely chopped
1 tsp cayenne
½ tsp Tabasco
USA long-grain rice (amount as required for 4-6 servings)

1 Make the brown roux: in a cast-iron skillet or heavy-bottomed pan, mix the flour and the oil to a smooth paste. Cook over a low heat for about 45 minutes, stirring constantly, until the mixture turns a rich dark brown and begins to give off a lovely nutty smell. Do not let it burn! (Some Cajun cooks brown the flour slightly first by toasting it in the oven, or under the grill.)
2 Prepare the chicken, removing the giblets, etc. In a very large stewing pot, place the chicken, whole, with the red peppers, bay leaves, thyme and salt, in as much water as it takes to cover completely. Cook, simmering, for about 30 minutes.
3 Prepare the vegetables.
4 Remove the chicken from the pot, skin and cut into serving portions.
5 Strain the stock, and reserve.
6 Transfer the roux to the very large pan, warm through, and add the garlic and onion. Cook until tender and add the okra and green pepper, mixing well. Gradually add the chicken stock, pouring into the roux in a slow stream, and stirring constantly. Finally, add the cayenne, Tabasco and the chicken pieces. Bring to the boil, reduce heat and simmer for about 1 hour.
7 Boil the rice (for traditional Cajun method, see chapter introduction).
8 Serve in warmed bowls – put some rice in each bowl, then ladle the gumbo over it, and add a piece of chicken on top.

Overleaf: Chicken gumbo

Dirty rice

Serves: 2 as a main dish. The same amount makes a starter for 6, or a side dish for 4.
225 g/8 oz chicken livers and 225 g/8 oz giblets
or 450 g/1 lb chicken livers (we used frozen)
2-3 medium-large onions, coarsely chopped
1 medium-large green pepper, chopped
1 stick celery, chopped
2 tbsp vegetable or corn oil
1 tsp salt
½ tsp black pepper
225-350 g/8-12 oz USA long-grain rice
water
3-4 tbsp fresh parsley, chopped

'Called 'Dirty Rice' because of its appearance, this tangy dish was tremendously well received when we tried it on friends. Don't be tempted to do without the parsley (and don't use dried) – it is really needed to set off the tastes. Although traditionally eaten as a main or side dish, it makes an excellent and unusual starter, served on a bed of lettuce, and garnished with lemon wedges. '

1 If using frozen livers, allow to thaw. Clean the giblets, and prepare the vegetables.
2 Put the giblets, livers, onions, green pepper and celery into a blender, and give about a 10-second whizz. At this stage, it looks like liver soup – don't panic!
3 Heat oil in a heavy-bottomed pan (preferably cast iron, with a lid – you could use a heavy frying pan with lid). Add the puréed liver mixture, and salt and pepper. Stir the mixture gently, rather as you would cook scrambled eggs. When it has solidified, and resembles minced meat in texture, reduce heat to low and cook for about 45 minutes, with the lid on, or until the mixture turns a darker, richer brown.
4 While the liver mix is cooking, boil the rice (see the chapter introduction).
5 When the rice has absorbed all the water and is soft, remove from the heat, and turn out on to heated serving dish.
6 Add the liver mixture to the rice, and toss in the chopped parsley. Mix all together, gently fluffing the rice with a fork, allowing the liver granules to coat the rice grains. Serve immediately.

Shrimp creole

Serves: 4.
about 550 g/1½ lb shelled prawns
2 medium onions, chopped
1 large green pepper, chopped
2 sticks celery, chopped
4 cloves garlic, crushed
120 ml/4 fl oz cooking oil
2 × 400 g/14 oz cans tomatoes
120 ml/4 fl oz water
2 tbsp cornflour mixed with 2 tbsp water
2 bay leaves
1 tsp cayenne pepper
1 tbsp salt
1 tbsp paprika
pinch of thyme
dash of Tabasco
225 g/8 oz USA long-grain rice

'A richly colourful and spicy dish that is deceptively quick and easy to put together. It can be made in advance, as it reheats well. '

1 Prepare the vegetables.
2 Pour the oil into a saucepan, or a cast-iron or enamelled casserole dish, and heat gently. Add the onions, pepper, celery and garlic, and sauté gently for a few minutes to soften.
3 Add the tomatoes and their juice, add the water and the cornflour/water mix. Stir in well. Bring to the boil, stirring, and allow to boil for a few minutes, before reducing heat to simmer for 5 minutes or so.
4 Add seasonings, and then the prawns. Cover and simmer for 20-30 minutes.
5 While the Creole sauce is cooking, boil the rice (see chapter introduction).
6 Serve hot over rice.

Red beans and rice

This very simple and inexpensive dish is traditionally served every Monday in restaurants (and homes as well) in New Orleans. It is a thick, hearty dish – a real 'winter warmer'. Our taster's comment: 'Very comforting!' As a variation, you can add chunks of spicy continental sausage – grill it first.

Serves: 4-6.

450 g/1 lb dried red kidney beans
water for soaking plus 1.7 l/60 fl oz
1 bunch spring onions, with tops, finely chopped
1 medium onion, fairly coarsely chopped
½ medium green pepper, finely chopped
2 cloves garlic, crushed
85 g/3 oz butter or margarine
1 tsp white sugar
1 tsp salt
2 tsp black pepper
1 tsp cayenne
1-2 bay leaves
2 dashes Tabasco
Gammon or ham, piece any size between about 225 g/8 oz and 900 g/2 lb
225-350 g/8-12 oz USA long-grain or Patna rice

1 Soak the dried red kidney beans in water for several hours or overnight. Drain, and set aside in 1.7 l/60 fl oz water.
2 Prepare the spring onions, onion, pepper and garlic. (If wished, reserve a tablespoon of spring onion tops for garnish.)
3 Melt the butter/margarine in a large pot. Add the vegetables and garlic, and stirring now and then, cook until translucent.
4 Add the beans and their water, sugar, all seasonings, and the piece of gammon, whole. Bring to the boil. Red kidney beans contain a toxic substance (a trypsin inhibitor). To remove this, it is essential to boil the beans vigorously for the first 10 minutes of cooking time. Then reduce the heat and simmer for 2½-3 hours, adding more water if necessary.
5 During the last half-hour, either mash some beans against the side of the pot, or remove perhaps one-eighth of mixture and blend to a smooth paste, returning to the pot to thicken the gravy.
6 Remove the piece of gammon, dice into 1 cm/½ in cubes, and return to the pan. Cook through over a gentle heat.
7 Cook the rice (for the traditional Cajun method, see chapter introduction).
8 Serve the beans over the rice, and garnish with sprinkling of spring onion tops.

Shrimp and ham jambalaya

'An easy dish, tasty and filling, and relatively inexpensive. The traditional jambalaya is not fiercely hot; it's a moist rice dish something akin to a risotto. The first impression is of a light but quite subtle flavour, with a spicy aftertaste. It should be eaten immediately; or when cold, in which case the addition of a simple vinaigrette makes it into a delicious rice salad. It does not reheat well, losing much of its subtle colouring and flavour.

For an alternative version, you can substitute chopped chicken pieces for the prawns. '

Serves: 4.
225 g/8 oz shelled prawns
115 g/4 oz gammon or salt pork, cut into 1cm/½ in cubes
2 medium-large onions, chopped quite finely
1-2 sticks celery, diced
1 small green pepper, diced
3 cloves garlic, crushed
1-2 tbsp vegetable or corn oil
225 g/8 oz USA long-grain rice
about 600 ml/20 fl oz water
1-2 bay leaves
1 tsp salt
½ tsp black pepper
1 tsp cayenne
4 dashes Tabasco

1 If using frozen prawns, allow to thaw. Chop the gammon/pork and prepare the vegetables.
2 Using a large, preferably cast-iron pot (with a lid), put in the oil, and heat. Add the onions, celery, green pepper and garlic. Stir, and add the rice. Cook, stirring occasionally, for about 10 minutes, or until the vegetables soften and the rice begins to brown.
3 Add about 150 ml/5 fl oz water, and bring to the boil. Add the prawns, gammon and all the seasonings. Add the remaining water and bring to the boil again. Cover, reduce the heat, and simmer until the rice is cooked (about 20 minutes).
4 Adjust the seasoning to taste. Serve immediately.

Right: Shrimp and ham jambalaya

Redfish courtbouillon

'This dish has the consistency of a very thick soup or stew. Redfish is often hard to find, and we've tried using snapper, but found it too bony. However, any firmly meaty and non-oily white fish will do: cod tasted just fine. To make the fish stock, try to get cod pieces – either shoulder or trimmings – from your fishmonger. **,**

Serves: 6.
1.25 kg/2½ lb redfish, cut into 7.5 × 2.5 cm/3 × 1 in strips
fish trimmings for stock
300 ml/10 fl oz water
6 tbsp brown roux (see recipe for Chicken gumbo on page 17)
1 medium onion, finely chopped
1 stick celery, finely chopped
3-4 large spring onions, finely chopped
2 green peppers, finely chopped
2 × 400 g/14 oz cans tomatoes
225 g/8 oz tomato purée
1-2 large bay leaves
½ tsp thyme
½ tsp marjoram
¼ tsp allspice
1 tsp cayenne
2 tbsp lemon juice
120 ml/4 fl oz dry white wine

1 Make the fish stock by simmering fish pieces in about 300 ml/10 fl oz water.
2 In a large enamelled casserole or cast-iron pan, make the roux. When it has browned, add the onion, celery, spring onions and garlic, and cook until soft. Add the green peppers.
3 Drain the canned tomatoes, reserving the juice. Chop the tomatoes and add to the roux, along with the tomato purée, and stir well. Add the strained fish stock, and stir well.
4 Now season with the herbs and spices, and the lemon juice. Cook on medium heat, stirring occasionally, until the mixture is fairly thick and firm enough to hold its shape in a spoon.
5 While the sauce is cooking, prepare the fish. Cut into strips, and add to the sauce.
6 Now add the wine, reduce the heat and simmer very gently (cover the pan) for 20 minutes or so, until the fish pieces are cooked. Adjust the seasoning and serve at once.

Pompano en papillote

This famous New Orleans dish is well worth the effort for that special occasion – though the effort is less than it may seem when you first read the recipe! But part of the fun lies in its presentation. It is extremely difficult to get pompano: we have tried snapper, but feel it's too bony for this dish. Plaice or sole is far more successful, but you could use any firm white fish – try John Dory, bass or turbot – and some recommend trout as an alternative. Get some fish trimmings for the stock at the same time.

Serves: 6.
3 pompano, filleted
225 g/8 oz shelled prawns
fish trimmings for stock
750 ml/25 fl oz water, lightly salted
1 lemon, sliced
1 tsp thyme
1 bay leaf
1 onion, finely chopped
2-3 large mushrooms, finely chopped
5-6 crab sticks
50-85 g/2-3 oz butter or margarine
3 tbsp flour
¼ tsp salt
2 egg yolks
baking parchment, or greased brown paper

1 If using frozen prawns, set to thaw. Preheat the oven to 200°C/400°F/Gas Mark 6.

2 Make the fish stock: to the lightly salted water add the fish trimmings, lemon slices, thyme, and bay leaf, and bring to the boil, then lower heat to simmer.

3 Rinse and pat dry the fillets. Lay out pieces of baking parchment (or greased brown paper) large enough to form a parcel for each fillet. Cut each paper into an oval and fold in half, placing the fillet on one half, near the centrefold. Fold over the top of the paper, and fix by folding edges together. Starting at one end, turn in edges about 5 mm/¼ in and fold, then fold again, and continue around edge until all is sealed by a doublefold.

4 Prepare the vegetables. Finely chop the prawns and crab sticks.

5 Remove the fish stock from the heat, and strain.

6 Melt the butter/margarine in a saucepan. Add the flour, stirring all the time, and allow to cook through for 2-3 minutes, before adding the onion. Cook until it is lightly browned.

7 Gradually add the fish stock to the roux, using as much as is necessary to achieve a fairly thick coating of sauce. Stir well, and cook for a further 5 minutes or so, until the sauce thickens. Add the prawns, crab meat, and mushrooms, with the salt, and mix well, heating through gently.

8 Remove the sauce from the heat, and stir in the beaten egg yolks. Spoon the sauce over each fillet, and wrap into a parcel, place on baking trays or in shallow tins or dishes, and bake in the centre of the oven for about 20 minutes.

9 Remove from the oven, and place the unopened parcels on each plate. Serve as they are, or, if you prefer, unfold the parcel and peel back the paper just as you are ready to present the dish at the table. The fish should not be removed from the paper. We think it's better to serve the parcels unopened – unwrapping your own is part of the fun, and the escaping aroma as you do so adds to the anticipation of delight.

Bread pudding with whiskey sauce

A rather special version of the old favourite, well known to us – very filling, but very moreish!

The sauce keeps for several months – that is, if you can resist the temptation! – just reheat gently. If you haven't any bourbon, you can use Scotch (we've even made it with brandy which tasted good if unauthentic – but it won't be Cajun).

Serves: 8-10.
Pudding:
350 g/12 oz day old French or Italian white bread (baguettes are good)
1.2 l/40 fl oz milk
3 eggs
450 g/1 lb granulated sugar
85 g/3 oz raisins
teaspoons? ———— 2 tbsp vanilla essence
Sauce:
115 g/4 oz butter or margarine
225 g/8 oz granulated sugar
1 egg
120 ml/4 fl oz bourbon

1 Preheat the oven to 180°C/350°F/Gas Mark 4. Grease a 23 × 30 cm/9-12 in baking dish.
2 Break the bread into chunks and place in a mixing bowl. Pour the milk over the bread and let it soak. When soft, crumble the bread into smaller pieces.
3 Beat the eggs and the sugar with a wire whisk, until smooth and thick. Stir in the raisins and the vanilla essence. Now add the egg mixture to the bread and mix well.
4 Pour the mixture into the greased baking dish, and put this dish into a large, shallow roasting pan. Pour boiling water into the outer pan, to a depth of 2.5 cm/1 in. Bake for 1 hour.
5 Meanwhile, make the sauce: melt the butter/margarine in the top of a double boiler, over hot (but not boiling) water.
6 Beat the egg with the sugar, and add to the butter/margarine, stirring constantly for 2-3 minutes until the sugar has dissolved. Do *not* let it boil or the sauce will curdle.
7 Remove from the heat, cool to room temperature before adding the bourbon. If wished, warm through again gently, and serve with the hot pudding.

Bananas foster

This dessert looks rich, and tastes pretty rich too. Created at Brennan's, a famous New Orleans restaurant, for one of its best patrons, this dish is still a house speciality, but has now become a regional favourite too. It is very easy to do – if you haven't the re-quisite table-top alcohol burner, use a frying pan on the hob. The dish tastes as good, and if you can carry it to the table while still aflame, it will be almost as impressive!

Serves: 4.
4 bananas, firm but ripe
115 g/4 oz butter, cut into smallish pieces
115 g/4 oz brown sugar (soft brown, molasses or muscovado, but not demerara)
vanilla ice cream
½ tsp ground cinnamon
120 ml/4 fl oz white rum or one part white rum, one part banana liqueur

1 Peel the bananas and halve them lengthways. Measure out all ingredients and have them to hand.
2 Light the alcohol burner/table-top stove, and set a large 30 cm/12 in, preferably copper, flambé dish over the flame.
3 Melt the butter in the pan, and add the sugar, stirring gently until you have a smooth syrup.
4 Add the banana halves, laying them gently in the pan. Cook gently for 3-4 minutes, basting often with the syrup.
5 While the bananas are heating through, place scoops of ice cream into individual serving dishes.
6 Sprinkle the bananas with cinnamon. In a ladle, gently warm the rum and add to the bananas. Ignite. Gently slide the contents of the pan around until the flames die.
7 Serve two banana halves on each plate of ice cream, and spoon syrup over the lot.

Cherries jubilee

Serves: 4.
1 × 785 g/1¾ lb tin black cherries
50 g/2 oz caster sugar
225 g/8 fl oz brandy
vanilla ice cream

This is simple and quick to do – and the pleasure in eating rich, hot cherries blended with cold, velvety ice cream . . . wonderful! The brandy undercuts the sweetness and gives a lovely boozy taste. Easy, yes, but special too!

1 Drain the cherries, reserving the juice. Pit the cherries if you prefer, but leave them whole.
2 For maximum effect, this should be cooked at the table, but can be done just as well on the hob in the kitchen. You do need to be fairly speedy, so have everything ready, measured out and standing to hand before you begin. If cooking at the table, light the alcohol burner, and allow the pan to heat through gently.
3 Pour the cherry juice into the pan, and add the sugar. Add the cherries, and stir gently, allowing the fruit to heat through and the sugar to melt.
4 While this is heating, scoop ice cream into serving bowls (about 2 scoops per serving).
5 Warm the brandy gently in a separate pan, or in a large ladle. Gently add the brandy to the cherries, stir, and ignite. Once the flames have died, spoon the fruit and juice over the ice cream and serve at once.

Calas (Rice cakes)

Makes: about 50. If you don't need so many, make a half-batch.
225 g/8 oz USA long-grain or Patna rice
about 750 ml/25 fl oz water
225 g/8 oz plain flour
2 tsp baking powder
¼ tsp salt
175-225 g/6-8 oz sugar (granulated or caster)
4 eggs, separated
150 ml/5 fl oz milk
icing sugar

These are very similar to drop scones (griddle scones or Scotch pancakes), but perhaps smaller. In New Orleans, they are often served with café au lait. If you have a griddle, use it – it's ideal. Otherwise, a heavy frying pan will suffice.

1 Add the rice to the water, and cook. When soft, drain, rinse, and drain again. Cool the rice. (Don't worry if you overcook the rice – this is all right for rice cakes.)
2 In a large mixing bowl, sift the flour with baking powder and salt. Add the sugar, and mix well.
3 Separate the eggs. Beat the yolks, add the milk, and blend well.
4 Add the egg mixture to the dry ingredients, mix well to a thick batter.
5 Whisk the egg whites until foamy, and leave to rest while you add the rice to the batter, and mix together well.
6 Beat the egg whites again until fairly stiff, and gently fold into the batter.
7 Heat a lightly oiled griddle or frying pan, and drop small portions of batter onto it – use a dessertspoon or tablespoon. (They should not be too large – a dessertspoon is about right.) The batter will spread a little into a sort of circle. The cakes are flattish, and, as they cook, bubbles form on the surface. When more or less set, turn the cakes and let them brown on the other side. Keep a brush and some oil to hand – you will probably need to recoat the griddle with a thin film every so often to prevent the calas from sticking.
8 Remove, and dredge with icing sugar. Eat hot. If you serve them immediately they are delicious – try a squirt of lemon juice, or some fruit syrup. A good fruity jam is a favourite accompaniment too. They're almost as good cold – the sugar melts a bit and resets, giving the cakes a different texture. Stored while still warm in an airtight container, you will find that the sugar turns to syrup – this keeps the calas moist, and is rather delicious. As a change from the traditional calas, you could add some flavouring to the batter – try vanilla, or lemon, or perhaps some raisins.

Beignets

Makes: 35-40.
150 ml/5 fl oz lukewarm water
5 tsps dried active yeast
115 g/4 oz granulated sugar plus 1 tsp
85-115 g/3-4 oz butter or margarine
1 tsp salt
150-175 ml/5-6 fl oz boiling water
300 ml/10 fl oz double cream
2 eggs, lightly beaten
900 g/2 lb – 1 kg/2¼ lb plain flour, plus flour to dust rolling surface
oil for deep frying
icing sugar – lots!

'Beignets are akin to doughnuts, but we have yet to discover a 'polite' way of eating them. It's icing sugar – everywhere! But don't be inhibited – they are far too delicious to worry about such niceties. Tuck in, and enjoy, with a cup of good strong coffee. (And, in the unlikely event of you having any left over, they are still scrumptious cold!)

If you prefer to make fewer, simply halve the ingredients. However, you will find a large batch of hot beignets perfect for a coffee morning, or when you have a horde of hungry kids to feed.

In New Orleans, near the French Quarter, there are large coffee houses which serve only coffee and beignets. Tourists and locals alike go there anytime of the day or night for the experience – and one always waits for a seat!

Beignets are fairly easy to make, and it is perfectly possible to cook them single-handed, but if you can co-opt an under-chef to stand by with the icing sugar, the task is quicker and simpler. Allow about 30 minutes for preparation, but the cooking time depends on how many you do in one batch. **,**

1 Put the lukewarm water into a bowl, sprinkle in the yeast, leave for a couple of minutes, then add 1 teaspoon sugar, and mix. Remove the bowl to a warm place and leave the yeast mixture to froth up (10-15 minutes).
2 Meanwhile, put the granulated sugar, butter/margarine, and salt in a large mixing bowl. Add the boiling water and stir until all the fat is melted and the mixture blended. Set aside to cool a little – it should be lukewarm for the next step.
3 When the yeast mixture is ready, add it to the butter mixture along with the cream, and the beaten eggs. Mix gently but well.
4 Now gradually add about 450 g/1 lb flour, mixing in well. When this is blended, add the remaining flour, gradually, working the dough until it is smooth and has lost its stickiness. (The amount of flour you need is not fixed.)
5 Heat the oil in a deep fryer.
6 Halve the dough and, on a well-floured surface, roll out the first batch into a large rectangle, no thicker than 3-5 mm/⅛-¼ in. Cut into 10×5 cm/4×2 in rectangles. (If you have the space, you can roll out all the dough at once, but we think it's easier to handle two batches.)
7 When the oil is hot enough, drop in a beignet. After a few seconds, the dough should bob to the surface, and puff up. Turn it over, and continue to fry for another 3 minutes or so, until it is a rich golden brown. It should be golden crisp on the outside, and springy soft inside, perhaps slightly 'doughy', but not raw! We suggest you break into it to check that it is cooked through. Be prepared for the first one to be a dud – if the oil is not hot enough, you'll get an anaemic and somewhat leaden beignet which flops about, soaks up too much oil, and won't puff. If the oil is too hot, you'll get a wonderfully puffy, rich brown beignet with a hot runny raw centre – and if the oil is hotter still, your beignet will be black! When you have the oil at the right temperature, you can do 2-3 at a time, depending on the size of the pan – they need space enough to rise and puff.
8 When the beignets are cooked, remove from the oil, and drain on kitchen paper. (If you are doing the dough in two batches, watch the oil to make sure it doesn't overheat.)
9 Dredge the beignets with sifted icing sugar. (Now is the time to have your mate standing by!) Forget all notions of the sort of gentle sprinkling you might give the top of a Victoria Sandwich – beignets should be *deluged* with icing sugar, both sides, and, as you pile them on to a warmed serving plate, add even more for good measure! Serve while hot.

Mardi Gras King's cake

50 g/2 oz butter or margarine
1 pkt dried active yeast
85 ml/3 fl oz lukewarm water
50-85 g/2-3 oz granulated sugar plus 1-2 tsp
275 g/10 oz plain flour plus extra flour for kneading
1 tsp salt
½-¾ whole nutmeg, grated
grated rind of 1 lemon
3 egg yolks
85 ml/3 fl oz warmed milk
50-115 g/2-4 oz sultanas/raisins/chopped glacé cherries
Glaze:
1 egg
1 tbsp milk
Icing:
icing sugar
lemon juice
hot water
6 tbsp granulated sugar
food colourings – purple, yellow and green

❝Mardi Gras – one of the world's most famous carnivals! The season begins just after Christmas with balls and parties, steadily intensifying until Fat Tuesday (in French, *mardi gras*) – Mardi Gras Day. Unlike most Southerners, the New Orleanians tend to be Catholic, so Mardi Gras is a true Carnival – a farewell to meat – for this leads to Lenten fasting. The King's cake is part of the tradition. At every party there will be such a cake, to be divided between the guests. A small bean or doll is baked into the cake, and the person getting the slice with the token must then have another party, with a King's cake . . . and so on, until Mardi Gras Day. The icing is in traditional Mardi Gras colours of purple, gold and green, which symbolize justice, power and faith.

We have left out the bean, or doll, but if you want to keep the tradition alive, incorporate it into the dough with the fruit. If you want to make a larger cake (or two small ones) just double the quantities, but we suggest that you use only 5 eggs, and 5 fl oz warmed milk.

This makes a good coffee-morning cake, late-night snack cake, and for those who aren't keen on the usual rich gateau creations, it can be served as a birthday cake. It certainly looks festive enough! ❞

1 Allow the butter/margarine to soften, and cut into smallish pieces. Set aside.
2 Put the contents of the packet of yeast into about 85 ml/3 fl oz lukewarm water, add 1-2 teaspoons sugar, stir, cover with clean cloth, and place in a warm place for about 10-15 minutes, until the yeast has frothed and increased in volume.
3 Into a large mixing bowl, sift 225 g/8 oz flour with 50-85 g/2-3 oz sugar, 1 teaspoon salt, the grated nutmeg, and the lemon peel, and mix well.
4 Separate the eggs. Warm 85 ml/3 fl oz milk. When the yeast mixture is ready, remove from the warmth and add to the flour mix. Add the egg yolks, and the milk, and mix well, until all the dry ingredients are thoroughly incorporated. When the mixture is as smooth as you can make it, begin to add the small pieces of butter, gradually mixing in all 50 g/2 oz. Continue to work the dough until it can be formed into a medium-soft ball.
5 Place the dough on a generously floured surface, knead well, mixing in another 50 g/2 oz flour (though you may have to add more to get the right consistency). Work the dough until it is no longer sticky. Continue kneading for about another 10 minutes, until the dough is smooth and elastic. Grease the inside of a large bowl, place the dough in it, cover, and set to rise in a warm place (1-1½ hours).
6 While the dough is rising, prepare the fruit – chop cherries, plump sultanas, etc. Prepare the coloured sugars by mixing into 2 tablespoons granulated sugar a few drops of purple food colouring. If you are careful not to add too much colouring, you will find that the sugar takes on the colour without dissolving. Repeat with the other colours, and set each aside on a separate saucer. Grease a baking sheet or a 23 cm/9 in ring mould.
7 When the dough has risen remove from warmth. Knock down, turn onto a floured surface and knead again, this time incorporating the fruit. Form the dough into a cylinder, and either place on a baking sheet, looping it round to form an oval ring, and pinching the ends together, or place the dough into the ring mould. Cover and set to rise again (about 45 minutes).
8 Preheat oven to 190°C/375°F/Gas Mark 5.
9 Beat the egg and milk to form the glaze. When the dough has risen, brush the top and sides of the cake with the glaze. If you are using a ring mould which turns out upside down, rather than a springform pan, you cannot glaze the top of the cake, so omit this stage – no matter.
10 Bake for 20-25 minutes, centre oven.
11 Remove and allow to cool.
12 Prepare the icing by sifting the icing sugar. Then mix it with the juice of a lemon, and just enough water to give a gently runny consistency. Pour on top of the cake allowing it to dribble down the sides. This should not be a heavy layer of icing, but we have found it necessary sometimes to spoon on another thin layer.
13 Quickly, before the icing sets at all, sprinkle the coloured sugars on to the icing in bands of purple, yellow and green.

Overleaf: Mardi Gras King's cake

2.

The Southwest

Tex-Mex
Fare

*Y*ou are now arriving in 'cowboy country' and believe it or not, cowboys do still exist – not in the gun-slinging John Wayne-style, movie version, but in the form of the ranch owner or hand. In the early settler days it was believed that sheep and cows could not be reared together, because if they grazed the same land the sheep would leave nothing for the cows. The ranchers opted for cows, and cows it's been ever since. The ranches may cover vast areas, so for the cowboys minding the cattle is often a rather isolated job, and because the day is long and physically hard they work up a fearsome appetite. They hit town, in their boots and ten-gallon hats (though minus spurs and six-guns) to stoke up on food and have a wild time.

This is real beef-eating country and steak restaurants are thick on the ground. The portions are incredibly large – I've certainly never been able to finish an entire serving but, since for Americans, carrying out leftovers in a 'doggybag' is an accepted custom, I've on occasion enjoyed steak and eggs for breakfast the next morning! As we've all had steaks, roasts, etc., (it's the size and possibly the quality that make the difference), we've decided not to include those recipes. There is, however, another very strong influence: that of the Mexicans.

You may remember from your history lessons that Texas was once a part of Mexico. Now that Texas is a state of the Union, Mexican Americans, who are known as 'Chicanos', have brought their cuisine into the USA, where it has been enthusiastically adopted (and adapted) by Americans. Mexican food is now popular throughout the States. The best is to be found in the Southwest and in California (and I've probably insulted the Californians by including it in this chapter).

Mexican cooking as I know it, and as we present it here, is not pure Mexican at all, but a rather adulterated version, commonly called Tex-Mex. Ten years ago, when I went on holiday to Cancun Mexico, my mouth watering all the way for what I thought of as Mexican food, I was sorely disappointed – it was nowhere to be found until I returned to the Southwest! The food can be richly spicy and very hot, due to the use of chillies and jalapeno peppers but, as with Asian food, much depends on the quantity of spices used. Don't be afraid to try, but go gently on the peppers until you've built up a tolerance.

Lastly, you will find a number of zucchini (courgette) recipes. I lived for a time in Denver, the 'mile-high city', where the growing season is short but everybody seemed able to produce zucchini and squash in abundance. I never grew them myself but each year I was given bushels. We all got extremely creative in finding different ways to prepare them. Try a few!

Salsa fria

"A sauce or dip which can really make your eyes water! Don't be too alarmed – the ferocity is calmed by eating it with corn chips. Very popular in Mexican restaurants, where the rule seems to be the hotter the better!"

Makes: about 450 ml/15 fl oz.
2 medium-large tomatoes, skinned and chopped
1 × 200 g/7 oz can tomatoes, with juice
1 small onion, finely chopped
1-2 sticks celery, finely chopped
¼ green pepper, finely chopped
115 g/4 oz can whole green chillies, chopped
1 tbsp olive oil
1 tbsp red wine vinegar
¼ tsp dry mustard
½ tsp ground coriander
½ tsp salt
dash black pepper

1 Skin tomatoes by placing them in just-boiled water for a minute or so. Make a slit in the skins and wait – they will practically peel themselves. Drain, pulling off the remaining skin.
2 Chop all vegetables. Mix all ingredients together. In a blender, give the mixture a few seconds' whizz – you don't want it completely smooth, just slightly puréed.
3 Cover and chill for several hours.
Serving suggestions: serve with corn chips, as a dip, or as a sauce to accompany Mexican food. Salsa fria keeps well in a screw-top jar in the refrigerator. If you are into Mexican food, we recommend that you keep a stock handy – salsa fria can be used in any recipe which calls for taco sauce.

Guacamole

"One of the most famous Mexican side dishes, it is served as a topping for Burritos and Chalupas, and also makes a useful party dip – try it with corn chips.

Be careful not to make this too far in advance – after a few hours the avocado begins to discolour."

Makes: 600 ml/20 fl oz.
4 large ripe avocados
1 medium tomato, peeled and finely chopped
1 medium mild green chilli, chopped
2 tbsp lemon juice
salt and pepper to taste
1 clove garlic, crushed
50-120 ml/2-4 fl oz sour cream (you could use a thick yoghurt)

1 Peel and stone the avocados, chop roughly and put into a mixing bowl.
2 Prepare the tomato and the chilli, and mix with the avocado, mashing it all together.
3 Add the remaining ingredients. Mix well and season to taste. If you prefer a smoother texture, you could use a blender; alternatively, you can just whizz up half the mixture so there are a few larger chunks remaining.
4 Serve as a side dish, or as a dip.

Right: Salsa fria and Guacamole

Nachos

'A very tasty fingerfood, good to serve with drinks – but eat it with friends or, since the method is a real ice-breaker, with some would-be friends!'

Serves: 4.
1 × 225 g/8 oz box Nachips
115 g/4 oz strong Cheddar, grated
115 g/4 oz mozzarella, grated
275 g/10 oz can jalapeno peppers
1 × 225 g/8 oz jar taco sauce (mild or hot, according to taste)

1 Using a fairly shallow baking tin, spread the chips in a single layer, overlapping to cover and form a base with no gaps.
2 Spread the grated cheese liberally over the chips and bake or grill until well melted.
3 Meanwhile drain and chop the jalapeno peppers.
4 Remove the nachos from the heat, spread the taco sauce on top of the melted cheese and sprinkle with chopped peppers. The peppers are very hot so if you think some will find them too much, arrange them so they don't cover the whole.
5 Serve immediately. To eat, you pull it apart – it may not be decorous, but it's quite fun!

Jalapeno bean dip

'Easy to prepare, this excellent, fairly spicy dip goes well with nachos or other corn chips or with crackers – and we love it on bread!'

Makes: about 1.2 l/40 fl oz.
225 g/8 oz dried pinto beans, soaked overnight
1 small onion, chopped
2 cloves garlic, chopped or crushed
1 tbsp cider vinegar
2-3 heaped tsp jalapeno peppers, chopped
1 tsp salt and ½ tsp black pepper
½ tsp paprika

1 Drain the soaked beans, and place in a saucepan, with fresh water to cover. Bring to the boil and cook until soft, adding a little water every now and then, to maintain the level.
2 Chop the onion, garlic, and the jalapeno peppers.
3 When the beans are very soft, remove from heat and cool slightly before placing in the blender goblet (with their liquid). Add the chopped onion and the garlic, with the cider vinegar, and blend to a purée.
4 Add the jalapeno peppers and the seasonings and leave to cool.

Beef jerky

Jerky is the name given to strips of oven-dried meat which are frequently packed by travellers, as a chewy and nutritious snack. In earlier days, it was part of the pioneers' food store, orginally venison, but nowadays usually made with beef. Having tasted the commercially-made Beef Jerky, we can honestly say that this home-made version is much better, a different thing altogether.

Makes: 40-50 strips.

900 g/2 lb lean beef (flank, steak, or brisket), partially frozen

Marinade:

1½ tsp meat tenderizer
1½ tsp seasoned salt
1½ tsp onion salt
½ tsp black pepper
1 clove garlic, crushed or ½ tsp garlic powder
50 ml/2 fl oz soy sauce
120 ml/4 fl oz Worcester sauce
salad oil

1 Slice the partially frozen meat into strips 2.5 cm/1 in wide by about 12.5 cm/5 in long, and about 3 mm/⅛ in thick.
2 Mix all the other ingredients (except the oil), and marinate the meat strips for at least 24 hours, in the refrigerator.
3 Remove the meat, drain well, and dry on absorbent paper.
4 Arrange the strips in a single layer on an oven rack. Place a sheet of foil at the bottom of the oven to catch the drippings. Set the oven at 70°C/150°F/Gas Mark 1 but leave the oven door open a crack. Bake the meat for about 7 hours, or until it is brittle but still chewy.
5 Remove the strips from the oven, and blot each one lightly with salad oil on a paper towel.
6 Store in an airtight container in the refrigerator. They will keep for about 6 months.

Chilli rellenos

This is typically a side dish for a Mexican meal, but also excellent as a starter. The relleno is something like a stuffed soufflé omelette, very mild in taste and with a delicious and unusual texture.

Makes: 12-15, to serve 6-7 people.

12-15 fresh long green medium-hot chilli peppers or 4 × 115 g/4 oz cans peeled whole green chillies
175-225 g/6-8 oz mature Cheddar (or half Cheddar, half mozzarella), grated
about 115 g/4 oz flour for coating plus 3 tbsp plain flour
6 eggs, separated
dash of salt
vegetable oil for frying
lettuce for garnish

1 Prepare the peppers: if using fresh, cut off tops, slit to open, and deseed. Blanch for a few seconds in boiling water and drain well. Pat dry. If using canned, drain and dry on kitchen paper, and remove any seeds.
2 Grate the cheese. In a shallow dish, put flour for coating.
3 Carefully fill each pepper with cheese, and roll gently in flour to coat well.
4 Separate the eggs. In a bowl, whisk the egg whites until they form stiff peaks. To the egg yolks, add 3 tablespoons flour and a dash of salt, and beat until the mixture is thick and golden-lemon in colour.
5 Fold the egg yolks into the egg whites.
6 Heat about 1 cm/½ in depth of oil in a frying pan. Test the heat with a drop of the egg mixture – it should be hot enough to sizzle immediately and retain its shape, without burning. For each relleno, spoon 2-3 tablespoons egg mixture into the oil and speedily shape into an oval. As the base begins to set, place a pepper on top and cover with 1-2 spoonfuls of the egg mixture. When the underside is golden, turn carefully, and cook the topside.
7 Remove and drain. Serve immediately, garnished with lettuce.

Tacos and tostadas

"'Taco' means 'snack', and is now the name commonly given to corn tortillas bent into a fillable 'shell'. Tostada is the flat version. Both taco and tostada shells are available in British supermarkets, and you can also buy cans of corn tortillas ready for frying. The fillings for both are a matter of choice (in the case of tostadas, the 'filling' is spread on top). **"**

Serves: 4-6.

1 dozen taco shells or 1 dozen tostada shells or 1 dozen corn tortillas (canned)
450 g/1 lb minced beef
1 tsp salt
1 tsp black pepper
1 tsp onion powder (optional)
1 clove garlic, crushed
1 packet taco seasoning mix (optional)
1 large onion, finely chopped
1 large tomato, finely chopped
½ small head iceberg lettuce, finely shredded
115-175 g/4-6 oz mature Cheddar, grated
1 × 225 g/8 oz jar taco sauce, hot or mild, according to taste

1 Place the minced beef in a pan, and, using no additional fat, brown the meat, adding the salt, pepper, garlic (onion powder and seasoning mix if used) and a handful of the chopped onion.
2 Stirring now and then, allow the meat mix to cook through. Meanwhile prepare the other ingredients and place in separate dishes.
3 When the meat is cooked, place in a serving dish, and keep hot.
4 If using prepared shells, heat in the oven according to packet directions (on a baking sheet, 5-10 minutes, at 180°C/350°F/Gas Mark 4). If using canned tortillas, heat oil about 1 cm/½ in deep, in a frying pan. Fry the tortillas for about 3 seconds per side, and place immediately on absorbent paper to drain.
5 Place all dishes on the table. While you could fill or top the tortillas in the kitchen, it's usual for guests to fill or spread their own, with a little bit of this or that, as they choose. Eat with your hands – messy but fun!

Huevos rancheros

"This is a hearty and hot brunch dish (or breakfast, if you have the stomach for it that early) – it goes rather well with Buck's Fizz! You could serve it for lunch, perhaps accompanied by a crisp green salad. **"**

Serves: 4.

2 chorizo (spicy pork) sausages, or about 225 g/8 oz weight
about 175 g/6 oz salsa fria (see recipe on page 34)
150 ml/5 fl oz tomato juice
1 bunch spring onions, finely chopped
12 black olives, pitted and chopped
1 tsp ground cumin
2 cloves garlic, crushed
50-115 g/2-4 oz Cheddar, grated
4 eggs
4 corn tortillas
vegetable oil for frying
1 lime or lemon, cut into wedges

1 Skin the chorizos, dice, and brown (using no additional fat) in a fairly deep frying pan (with a lid – you'll need it later).
2 Add the salsa fria, tomato juice, and about half the amount of spring onions and olives. Stir in the cumin and garlic, and simmer for about 20 minutes.
3 Meanwhile, grate the cheese.
4 Poach the eggs in the sauce: make a well for each egg, and gently break the egg into it. Cover and leave on low heat for about 10 minutes or until the eggs are cooked and the whites are properly set.
5 While the eggs are poaching, heat about 1 cm/1 in oil in a frying pan, drop in the corn tortillas and cook for a few seconds per side. They will crisp up. Remove and drain on absorbent paper. Place on a warmed serving dish.
6 On each tortilla lay an egg with sauce, and top with grated cheese, and a sprinkling of the remaining spring onions and olives. Serve with lime or lemon wedges.

Left: Vegetable burritos (recipe, page 40) and Chilli con carne (recipe, page 42)

Vegetable burritos

Makes: 6.
6 flour tortillas (see recipe on page 41)
Filling:
I small onion, thinly sliced
2 cloves garlic, crushed
I tbsp vegetable oil
I large tomato, skinned and chopped
I carrot, thinly sliced
I small-medium green pepper (capsicum, not chilli), sliced
2 medium courgettes, sliced
115 g/4 oz mushrooms, sliced
I tsp chilli seasoning
½ tsp salt
½ tsp dried oregano
¼ tsp ground cumin
175 g/6 oz Cheddar (or mixed with mozzarella), grated
Toppings:
guacamole (see recipe on page 34)
sour cream

6 For another variation, fill the tortillas with refried beans and grated cheese. Heat through in oven until the cheese has melted, and serve hot, with a topping of sour cream. For some reason, this one seems to go down well for breakfast! 9

1 Make the tortillas and set aside.
2 Chop the onion, and sauté, with garlic, in oil till soft.
3 Skin the tomato, and chop. Prepare the other vegetables and add all to the onion. Add the seasonings, and cook gently until all are tender.
4 Meanwhile, make the guacamole. Preheat the oven on a low heat.
5 Grate the cheese. When the vegetables are cooked, remove from heat and stir in the cheese.
6 Fill the tortillas, roll, and place in a shallow dish in the oven to heat through.
7 Serve hot, topped with a spoonful of guacamole or sour cream, or both.

Green chilli burritos

Makes: 6.
450 g/1 lb pork, fairly lean, diced in small cubes
350-450 ml/12-15 fl oz chicken stock (preferably homemade)
2 × 100 g/3½ oz can green chillies, chopped
3 small dried red chillies (optional)
I × 200 g/7 oz can tomatoes, drained and chopped
I tsp chilli seasoning
¼-½ tsp ground cumin
½ tsp oregano
I × 450 g/16 oz can refried beans or see recipe on page 48
6 flour tortillas (see recipe on page 41)
Toppings:
115 g/4 oz sharp Cheddar (or half Cheddar, half mozzarella), grated
¼ small head iceberg lettuce, shredded
2 tomatoes

6 Similar to enchiladas, burritos have a different filling and are served not with a sauce, but with toppings. There are several variations. 9

1 If making refried beans, do this first.
2 Dice pork and simmer in chicken stock (use 350 ml/12 fl oz to start with), and cook until tender.
3 Drain the green chillies, chop and add to the pork, along with the dried red chillies. Add the drained, chopped tomatoes. Cook for a further 20 minutes, adding seasoning, cumin and oregano.
4 If using canned beans, heat them through now.
5 Make the tortillas, or if you have previously done so, lay them out ready for filling. Lightly grease a shallow pan or dish, and preheat the oven at low-medium heat.
6 Spread a layer of beans on each tortilla, spoon on the pork mixture (use a slotted spoon to drain off excess moisture), and roll up the burritos. Place in the dish and put in the oven.
7 Grate the cheese, shred the lettuce, and chop the tomatoes.
8 Serve the burritos hot, with the cheese, lettuce and tomatoes as topping.

Enchiladas

Makes: 12.
12 flour tortillas (see recipe below)
Sauce:
25 g/1 oz butter or margarine
2-3 small onions, chopped
2 cloves garlic, crushed
1 × 400 g/14 oz can tomatoes
2-3 tbsp tomato purée, in about 120 ml/4 fl oz water
1 mild green chilli, chopped
1 tsp sugar
1 tsp ground cumin
½ tsp salt
½ tsp oregano
½ tsp basil
150 ml/5 fl oz sour cream
Fillings *(for 6 of each):*
Chicken: *2 medium chicken breasts, cooked, skinned, boned, and diced*
85-115 g/3-4 oz grated Cheddar
Cheese: *175-225 g/6-8 oz grated Cheddar*

◖Enchiladas are a sort of stuffed pancake topped with a delicious creamy tomato sauce. They can be very filling. **❯**

1 Make the sauce: melt the butter/margarine in a large frying pan, add the onions and garlic, and cook until tender. Add the tomatoes, with their juice, and the tomato purée in water. Mix in and add the chopped green chilli. Add all the seasoning and cook for about 20 minutes.
2 Prepare the fillings: grate the cheese, dice the chicken.
3 Make the flour tortillas.
4 When the sauce is cooked, remove from heat. Take a tortilla and, lay it on top of the sauce so that the underside is lightly covered. Turn over so that both sides get a slight coating.
5 Transfer the tortilla to a shallow bowl or flat surface. Place a handful of the chicken pieces and a spoonful of cheese on the tortilla, in a line that is more or less central. Fold, and roll, place in a pan (about 5 cm/2 in deep). Continue until you have filled and rolled all the tortillas. When making the cheese enchiladas, be generous with the filling.
6 Add the sour cream to the sauce, and pour the sauce over the enchiladas. Bake in the oven, for 40 minutes at 180°C/350°F/Gas Mark 4. Serve hot.
Note: Enchiladas do not reheat well, but they can be prepared the day before up to point of baking, and kept refrigerated.

Flour tortillas

Makes: 12.
450 g/1 lb plain white flour
1 tsp baking powder
1 tsp salt
1½ tbsp shortening (we use vegetable shortening)
175 ml/6 fl oz cold water

◖The tortilla, corn or flour, is a staple of Tex-Mex food. The corn tortilla can be bought in the UK, and is fine for Tacos, Tostadas, and Chalupas, but for Enchiladas and Burritos you really need flour tortillas which have a very different texture and pliability. They are something like an Indian chapati and can be filled and rolled easily. These flour tortillas are extremely simple to make and are, we think, far superior to the ready-made corn tortillas. They also have a more compatible taste. **❯**

1 Mix the dry ingredients, and cut in the shortening.
2 Add enough water to make a stiff dough (175 ml/6 fl oz is usually right), and knead until smooth. Divide the dough into 12 equal balls.
3 On a well-floured surface, roll out each ball into a thin circle 15 cm/6 in across. We find the simplest way of doing this is to use two fairly heavy duty plastic bags: flour one side of each bag, and roll out the balls between the bags.
4 Preheat a heavy griddle or frying pan over medium-high heat. Lightly grease the surface and bake each tortilla for ½-1 minute per side. Once cooked, set aside between layers of kitchen paper or tea towels. At this stage you can wrap the tortillas in foil and store in the fridge for use later – reheat (in their foil wrapping) in the oven.
5 The tortillas are now ready to be filled (see recipes for Enchiladas or Burritos, above and opposite) and rolled. Set in a dish and heat through in the oven. Serve hot.

Chalupas

‘A variation of the tostada, these tasty snacks are served on flat, crisp corn tortillas. ’

Serves: 4.
8 corn tortillas or tostada shells
Sauce:
I chicken breast, cooked, skinned, and shredded
450 g/I lb lean pork, cut into smallish cubes
2 tbsp vegetable oil
I tbsp plain flour
120 ml/4 fl oz water
2 cloves garlic, crushed
I × 200 g/7 oz can tomatoes, drained and chopped
I × 200 g/7 oz can green chillies, drained and chopped
I tsp ground cumin
I × 450 g/16 oz can refried beans or see our recipe on page 48 (amount is about same)
Toppings:
guacamole – (see recipe on page 34 – half the amounts given should suffice)
115 g/4 oz strong Cheddar, grated
150 ml/5 fl oz sour cream

1 If making refried beans, prepare the presoaked beans now, and make guacamole.
2 Put chicken to cook in whatever manner preferred. Meanwhile, brown the diced pork in the oil, and stir in the flour.
3 Add the water, garlic, tomatoes and chillies, and the cumin. Stir in well and simmer until the mixture has thickened. Keep warm.
4 When the chicken has cooked, skin and shred. Reheat beans if using the canned variety.
5 Heat the tostada shells in the oven, or, if using corn tortillas, fry in hot oil for about 3 seconds per side, and drain on absorbent kitchen paper.
6 To assemble the chalupas, layer onto each crisp tortilla the refried beans, then the shredded chicken, followed by the pork mixture, grated cheese, and a dollop of guacamole and sour cream.

Chilli con carne

‘This hearty and fiery-hot dish is so easy to make that you can (and Kenna did) teach a 5-year-old to make it; and it’s the one dish her children continue to make. What is or is not a good constituent of Chilli con carne seems to be a matter of controversy, engendering as much heat as the chilli itself (though it’s always worth getting good quality steak mince which is not fatty). So this is Kenna’s version, and very good it is too. ’

Serves: 4-6.
900 g/2 lb minced beef
275 g/10 oz dried red kidney beans, soaked overnight
or 2 × 425 g/15 oz cans red kidney beans
I medium-large onion, chopped
I green pepper, chopped
4-6 cloves garlic, crushed
I × 425 g/15 oz can tomatoes
10-15 tbsp tomato purée
8 tbsp chilli seasoning
2 tsp sugar
I tsp black pepper and 2 tsp salt

1 If using dried beans, soak overnight, then bring to boil in fresh water to which is added I tsp sugar. Red kidney beans contain a toxic substance. To remove this, it is essential to boil the beans vigorously for the first 10 minutes. Then low boil until the beans are soft. Drain, reserving some of the liquid.
2 In a large heavy-bottomed pan on a low heat, brown the meat. Add no fat, just stir now and then to prevent sticking.
3 Prepare the onion, pepper and garlic, and add to the meat. Mix in and cook until the vegetables are tender. If it is too dry add a dribble of water (or some of the bean liquid).
4 Add the beans: if using canned, you may like to add their liquid but, since Chilli can be as thick or as thin as you choose, you may prefer to adjust the consistency gradually. Add the tomatoes with their juice, and the tomato purée. Add all the seasonings, and more water if necessary.
5 Bring to the boil; reduce to simmer for at least 30 minutes. If it seems a bit sloppy, leave it uncovered. Stir now and then to prevent sticking.
6 Serve hot, over rice, or, as sometimes eaten in the Midwest, over noodles.

Right: Tacos and tostadas (recipe, page 39)

Puchero

'This is a thickish spicy pork and bean stew, with a rather piquant and unusual flavour. The flavour improves enormously with a lengthy cooking time, so do give yourself a few hours. '

Serves: 6.
225 g/8 oz dried pinto beans, soaked overnight
450 g/1 lb lean pork
1 large onion, sliced
1 large carrot, sliced
3 cloves garlic, crushed
1 tbsp oil
4 small dried red chillies
2 bay leaves
½ tsp black pepper
1 tbsp sugar
1-2 tbsp vinegar, (wine, not malt) (optional)
about 600 ml/20 fl oz water
2 chorizo (spicy pork) sausages
1 × 400 g/14 oz can tomatoes, drained

1 Drain the soaked beans. In fresh water, bring the beans to the boil, and cook for 1 hour, or until they begin to soften.
2 In a separate pan, place pork with water to cover, and bring to boil. Simmer for ¾-1 hour. Drain.
3 Slice the onions and carrots, and sauté with garlic in 1 tablespoon oil, in a large deep heavy-bottomed casserole dish, or heavy saucepan.
4 To the sautéed vegetables add the drained beans, the red chillies, bay leaves, pepper, sugar, and, if you like, the vinegar, which gives it a piquant taste. Add about 600 ml/20 fl oz water.
5 Cube the pork and add to the bean mix. Slice the chorizos and stir them in along with the drained tomatoes. Leave the stew to simmer gently for at least another hour, and much longer if you have the time. Add a little more liquid if necessary, and adjust the seasoning later. The longer it cooks, the better the different flavours will blend together – the spiciness of the chorizos needs time to permeate.
6 Serve hot. It is best eaten with some fairly bland accompaniment. We recommend that you eat it with cornbread (see recipe on page 145) – the puchero tastes good alone, but with the juices soaked into the cornbread, it's sensational!

Taco salad

'This is really more like a differently assembled taco than a salad as we understand it – nice for a change. The easy way to prepare the meat is with soup mix – if you prefer, you could cook the meat with some finely chopped onion, and seasonings of your choice. '

Serves: 4-6.
450 g/1 lb minced beef
1 pkt French onion soup mix
about 175 ml/6 fl oz cold water
1 × 200 g/7 oz jar taco sauce (mild or hot, to taste)
or salsa fria (see recipe on page 34)
1 small head iceberg lettuce, shredded
1 large tomato, sliced
1 small onion, sliced
½ small green pepper, chopped
about 12 black olives
85-115 g/3-4 oz Cheddar, grated
about 175 g/6 oz corn chips

1 Brown the minced beef, and sprinkle in the onion soup mix. Add the water, and taco sauce, and simmer for about 10 minutes.
2 Toss the rest of the ingredients (except corn chips) into a large salad bowl. When the meat is cooked, spoon it over the salad, and sprinkle the corn chips on top.

Colorado crustless quiche

'Not the least calorific meal in the book, but a good one to rustle up pretty quickly – but if you don't like cheese, move on; there's not much else in this. '

Serves: 4 as a light lunch or supper dish.
115 g/4 oz mozzarella
115 g/4 oz mild Cheddar
40-50 g/1½-2 oz soft cream cheese (Philadelphia is fine)
225 g/8 oz cottage cheese
50 g/2 oz butter or margarine
50 g/2 oz flour
3 eggs, beaten
½ tsp baking powder
½ tsp salt
½ tsp sugar
pinch of paprika or chilli

1 Preheat the oven to 180°C/350°F/Gas Mark 4.
2 Chop the mozzarella and the Cheddar into small cubes, and place in a mixing bowl.
3 Add the cream cheese and the cottage cheese, and mix.
4 In a saucepan, melt the butter/margarine, and stir in the flour, mixing gently to a smooth roux.
5 Add to the cheese mixture the 3 beaten eggs, baking powder, salt, and sugar, and mix well.
6 Add the roux, stir all together, and turn out into a fairly shallow baking dish. Add a sprinkling of paprika on top, or chilli if you like it hot. It's also a good dish for your favourite herbs – or you could mix in some mustard: try a teaspoon or two of a good French wholegrain sort. Place in the oven to cook for 45 minutes.

Texas hash

'A hearty meal, this, and a really handy one to have in your repertoire. Ideal for feeding the family, or for informal entertaining, it's very quick to prepare and practically cooks itself, thus leaving you free to be with your friends. Since it is possible to cook it all in one pot, it's great for bedsit cooking too.

The American recipe calls for chilli powder, but in the States this is a mixture of other seasonings too, so we recommend that you use what is sold here as 'chilli seasoning' (McCormick's). '

Serves: 4-6.
450 g/1 lb ground (minced) beef
2 large onions, sliced
1 medium-large green pepper, sliced
2 tbsp chilli seasoning
1½ tsp salt
½ tsp black pepper
1 × 400 g/14 oz can tomatoes plus 50 ml/2 fl oz water
85 g/3 oz long-grain white rice

1 Preheat the oven to 180°C/350°F/Gas Mark 4.
2 If possible, use a cast-iron casserole, or some other pan which can be used on the stove and in the oven. Set the pan on the heat, and brown the beef. Use no fat, and drain off any excess fat which appears.
3 Slice the onions and pepper, and mix with the meat. Add the seasonings, stir well, and cook until the vegetables are just tender.
4 Add the tomatoes with their juice and the additional water. Break them up to mix them in.
5 Stir in the uncooked rice.
6 Transfer the dish to the oven and cook for about 1 hour. It shouldn't be necessary to use a lid – the top gets nicely browned. If the rice is not fully cooked, add a little more liquid if necessary and give it a few minutes longer.
7 Serve immediately – it's really a one-dish meal but you could serve with extra vegetables or a salad if you felt the need.

Jan's zucchini dish

'We are indebted to Jan von Drehle, a green-fingered Colorado inhabitant who grew courgettes every summer, for this recipe. She usually served this as a side dish with barbecued steak or chicken. It is light, subtle, creamy and delicious, and makes a very adequate lunch or supper, served with a salad, or perhaps a baked potato. It is also a fine sauce for pasta, particularly good with spinach noodles. '

Serves: 4 as a side dish.
2-3 slices unsmoked bacon (streaky is fine)
4-6 medium-large courgettes
I medium onion, diced
I small cauliflower
225 g/8 oz cream cheese (Philadelphia is good)
I tsp salt
I tsp black pepper

1 Put a pan of water to boil. Cut the bacon into small pieces, add to the water, cover and low boil. If using smoked bacon, reduce the salt when you add seasoning.
2 Peel the courgettes and slice into rounds – not too thinly, about I cm/½ in. Add these to the pan, cover and low boil for about another 10 minutes.
3 Dice the onion, break the cauliflower into small florets.
4 Drain the courgettes, reserving about 150 ml/5 fl oz of liquid.
5 Return the courgettes and bacon to the pan with the reserved water. Add the onions and cauliflower.
6 Add the seasoning, and stir in the cream cheese.
7 Simmer gently for about 10 minutes, adjusting the consistency if necessary. It should be fairly thick, so if it seems a bit on the runny side, leave uncovered, to reduce.
8 Serve hot or cold.

Gwen's barbecued sweet corn

'Quite simply the most delicious way of cooking corn on the cob! Always buy it from a greengrocer because it must be in its husk. The prepared, prepackaged ones will not do. '

Serve: I cob per person.
corn on the cob – as many as you have mouths to feed
butter
salt

1 Pull out as much of the end silk as possible but leave each corn in its husk.
2 Soak the cobs in cold water for at least an hour.
3 On a charcoal grill, cook the corn, turning every now and then, for about 30 minutes. Remove the husks, roll the corn in melted butter, and salt to taste.

Zucchini casserole

'This seems to go well with most things, but perhaps particularly with fish. For vegetarians, it's an acceptable main dish – served with tomatoes, either baked or raw; mushrooms are good, too. '

Serves: 6-8 as a side dish.
4 medium courgettes, grated
115 g/4 oz Cheddar, grated
10 water biscuits, grated or crumbled
I small onion, grated or finely chopped
2 eggs, beaten
I tsp salt
½ tsp black pepper

1 Preheat the oven to 180°C/350°F/Gas Mark 4. Grease a casserole dish.
2 Grate into a mixing bowl the courgettes, cheese, crackers, and onion (use more onion if you like a stronger taste).
3 Add the eggs, and seasonings, mix all well together and turn out into the casserole. At this stage it looks like unappetizing slush, but don't worry! Pat it down into the dish, and bake for I hour. (It doesn't need a lid).

Right: Jan's zucchini dish

Refried beans (frijoles refritos)

❛Spoon some into tacos, spread on tostadas, or eat with burritos. This is really so simple and tastes *so* much better homemade. ❜

Serves: 6-8 as a side dish.
225 g/8 oz dried pinto beans, soaked overnight
I large onion, finely chopped
3 cloves garlic, crushed
I bay leaf
I tsp dried hot chillies
2 tsp salt or I tsp salt, I tsp onion salt
I tsp black pepper
2-3 tbsp oil for frying

1 Soak the beans overnight. Change the water, and bring to the boil. Cook for about I hour or until the beans are soft.
2 Prepare the onion and garlic, and add to the beans, with all the seasoning. Cook for a further 30 minutes or until the beans are very soft and mashable.
3 Drain the beans, and mash well.
4 Heat the oil in a frying pan, add the beans, patting down. Heat through and adjust seasoning. Cook until they seem a little drier. Serve hot.

Summer squash casserole

❛We don't have a wide variety of squash here, and we find this works equally well with pumpkin and marrow. The dish has a delicate flavour, good with chicken or fish. Kenna loves it as a light supper, served with brussels sprouts or broccoli. ❜

Serves: about 8, but the quantities can easily be halved.
900 g/2 lb yellow squash
I small onion, diced
I × 275 g/10 oz can condensed cream of chicken soup
300 ml/10 fl oz sour cream
2 large carrots, finely grated
2 × 85g/3 oz pkts herb stuffing mix
or about 175 g/6 oz fresh breadcrumbs
I tsp fresh parsley, chopped
½ tsp thyme or sage
salt and pepper to taste
115 g/4 oz butter or margarine, melted

1 Preheat the oven to 180°C/350°F/Gas Mark 4. Grease a casserole dish.
2 Peel the squash, and cut into small pieces. Dice the onion, and put both in a pan with just enough salted water to cover. Bring to boil, and cook for 5 minutes, or until soft enough to mash. Drain.
3 Mix the condensed soup with the sour cream, and beat till smooth. Add the squash and onion and mash together. Mix in the grated carrot.
4 Melt the butter/margarine, and stir into the breadcrumbs or the herb stuffing mix, to which the seasoning has been added.
5 Add the breadcrumbs or stuffing mix to the squash, and mix well. Turn out into the casserole dish and bake for about 30 minutes.
Note: This casserole keeps for a few days in the fridge, and can be reheated easily.

Sopaipillas

Makes: 12-15.
225 g/8 oz plain white flour
2 tsp baking powder
1 tsp salt
2 tsp vegetable shortening (solid vegetable oil)
150 ml/5 fl oz water
vegetable oil for frying
honey – the runny type is best

1 Sift all the dry ingredients together.
2 Add the shortening and the water. Mix and knead until the dough is soft and smooth (about 10 minutes). Place in a plastic bag, and refrigerate for 1-1½ hours.
3 Roll out the dough to about 3 mm/⅛ in thick, and cut into 5 cm/2 in squares.
4 Heat the oil in a deep frying pan – you need enough oil to cover the sopaipillas, say about 2.5 cm/1 in. Fry about 2 minutes per side. The sopaipillas should puff up – if they don't immediately, try increasing the temperature of the oil. They should be golden brown, and crisp outside. Drain on kitchen paper.
5 Serve hot. Slit one side, or break off a corner, and pour the honey into the bread pocket. Don't worry if they haven't all puffed well – you don't get a handy container for the honey, but they taste just as good with it spread on top!
Serving suggestions: If you aren't a honey lover, or you like a spicier taste, try rolling the cooked sopaipillas in cinnamon sugar. If it's a savoury you're after, you could mix some chilli seasoning powder with the dry ingredients. Another suggestion is to add, again at that early stage, a small amount of curry spices, and, cutting them into smaller squares, fry as before – these 'curry bites' are good with drinks.

'Mexican food is not usually divided into courses, but all put on the table together, so these delicious puffy breads are eaten with the meal. Since they ooze honey, this may not strike you as the best accompaniment to your Chilli or Tacos – we suggest that the more conservative among you keep them for a dessert. They are also delicious served with morning coffee. '

Sour cream cookies

Makes: 50-60.
350 ml/12 fl oz oil (vegetable or light salad oil)
350 g/12 oz brown sugar
4 eggs
2 tsp vanilla essence
450 g/1 lb plain flour
2 tsp bicarbonate of soda
½ tsp salt
300 ml/10 fl oz sour cream

1 Preheat the oven to 190°C/375°F/Gas Mark 5.
2 In a large mixing bowl, combine the oil with the sugar and stir well.
3 Add the eggs, and mix. Add the vanilla essence.
4 Sieve together the flour, soda, and salt, and add about a third of it to the mixture. Add some of the sour cream, and alternately add flour and sour cream until you have incorporated all the ingredients. Mix well.
5 With a teaspoon, drop small portions of the biscuit mixture onto baking trays (there is no need to grease them first). Allow room to spread – they should be about 3-5 cm/1½-2 in across when cooked.
6 Place in centre oven, and bake for 10-12 minutes. Remove from the oven but leave the biscuits on the tray for a few minutes before transferring to a cooling rack. Stored in an airtight container, these biscuits will keep for many weeks.
Serving suggestions: For a batch of Christmas cookies, we decided on a seasonal variation. We omitted the vanilla essence, and added instead, 2-3 teaspoons cinnamon, and 2 teaspoons allspice. The slightly chewy texture went rather well with the spiciness and they were a popular accompaniment to mid-morning coffee.

'Very simple and quick to mix, this is a good basic recipe for delicious cookies. They have a slightly unusual texture – neither soft, nor crisp, but a sort of chewy sponginess. '

Pina colada pie

❝This is a light and creamy dessert, easy to put together though not particularly economical if you don't keep white rum in stock. It is unusual, though, and well worth the cost for a special occasion. ❞

Crust:
225-275 g/8-10 oz digestive biscuits, crushed
about 175 g/6 oz butter or margarine
Filling:
1 × 400 g/14 oz can condensed milk
about 150 g/5 oz creamed coconut, grated or 1 × 350 ml/12 fl oz can Coco Lopez
50 ml/2 fl oz white rum
450 g/1 lb pineapple, fresh or canned, drained
300 ml/10 fl oz whipping cream
flaked coconut pieces as garnish (optional)

1 Lightly grease a 24 cm/9½ in dish or tin. Crush the biscuits to crumbs. We find the easiest way to do this is to put the biscuits into a plastic or greaseproof bag, and crush them with a rolling pin. This method will save you a lot of mess!

2 Melt the butter/margarine, and stir in the crumbs. When well coated, pat them down into the tin to form a base and sides. Chill while you make the filling.

3 In a mixing bowl, pour the condensed milk, and grate into it the coconut. Mix in and add the rum. Stir well. After a few minutes you will find the grated coconut begins to blend with the milk. (You can use a can of Coco Lopez creamed coconut rather than a grated block; its different consistency adds to the volume, so this would make enough filling for 2 large pies.)

4 Drain the pineapple if necessary and cut into small pieces. Add to the milk mixture.

5 In a large bowl, whip the cream until it has considerably increased in volume. Fold in the milk mixture. Pour into the pie shell and return to the fridge for at least 2-3 hours. Garnish with flaked coconut.

Right: Pina colada pie

Monkey bread

'This is a delicious, sweet bread, with a dough that is rather more like soft buns. In the US it is possible to buy cans of semi-baked dough which can be used for this bread, broken into balls and baked with layers of sugar and spices, nuts and raisins, or, in a savoury version, with lashings of grated cheese. Being unable to find any equivalent product here, we have at last discovered a recipe which turns out pretty much the same, but takes a little longer to prepare. '

1-2 medium potatoes, boiled, skinned and mashed
1 pkt active dried yeast
120 ml/4 fl oz warm water
120 ml/4 fl oz milk
115 g/4 oz white sugar
115 g/4 oz butter or margarine
2 tsp salt
2 eggs
450-550 g/1-1¼ lb strong white flour plus flour for kneading
Layering:
115 g/4 oz butter or margarine, melted
soft brown sugar, to taste
ground cinnamon, to taste
chopped pecan nuts or walnuts
raisins

1 Put the potatoes on to boil. When soft, drain, remove the skins and mash the potatoes as smoothly as you can. Set aside to cool.

2 Dissolve the yeast in the warm water, and gently warm the milk.

3 Add the yeast mixture and the milk to the mash, and stir in the sugar, salt and butter/margarine. Add the eggs and beat well. At this stage it looks quite awful – a sort of grey fatty swill. You may feel you'll never mix it properly, but it will be fine once you start adding the flour.

4 Beat in the flour a little at a time. It's helpful to use an electric beater at this stage, reverting to a spoon when the dough becomes too stiff. When you have added all the flour and the dough is ballable, turn out on to a floured surface and knead for about 10 minutes, incorporating as much extra flour as may be necessary to prevent it being sticky.

5 Place the dough in a lightly oiled bowl, cover, and leave in a warm place to rise, for about 1 hour.

6 Preheat the oven to 170°C/325°F/Gas Mark 3. Oil a 25 cm/10 in ring mould or a smaller round baking tin.

7 When the dough has risen punch it down again. You don't have to leave it to rise again. Melt the butter/margarine, and have lots of sugar and cinnamon ready, with the nuts and raisins to hand.

8 Pull the dough into smallish balls about the size of a ping-pong ball. You may find cutting it with a sharp knife is easiest. Roll the dough in your palms and drop into the tin. Continue until you have one layer. Pour half the melted butter over the dough balls, and then sprinkle with the sugar, cinnamon, nuts and raisins – be as generous as you can afford. Continue with another layer of dough balls, and top the layer, as before, with the rest of the butter, and with a really good amount of the toppings.

9 Bake for 45-50 minutes. The dough will rise up to fill the tin. Leave the bread in the tin until it has cooled a little. Eat warm, pulling the balls apart. If you are not eating it immediately (but how could you resist?), leave it to cool completely, remove, and wrap in foil. It keeps this way for about 4-5 days. Since it is best eaten warm, reheat gently in a low oven.

Zucchini bread

'If you grow your own courgettes, this is a particularly good recipe for using up the overgrown or even the tiny ones, and those past their peak. Don't be put off – it's a spicy sweet bread, similar to Carrot cake, and can be used in much the same way. If you want to ice it with Cream cheese frosting (for recipe see page 143), you can serve it as a dessert cake. '

3-4 medium courgettes
350 g/12 oz plain flour
350 g/12 oz granulated sugar
1 tsp bicarbonate of soda
1 tsp salt
1-2 tsp allspice
3 tsp cinnamon
1 tsp nutmeg, grated
1 tsp ground ginger
1 tsp ground cloves
175 ml/6 fl oz vegetable oil
3 eggs, beaten
3 tsp vanilla essence

1 Preheat the oven to 180°C/350°F/Gas Mark 4.
2 Wash but do not peel the courgettes. Grate them into a large mixing bowl.
3 Add all the dry ingredients and mix. The amounts of spices given above are only a guide – we like it well-spiced.
4 Add the oil, eggs and vanilla. When well blended, turn out into 2 greased, floured 900 g/2 lb loaf tins and bake for 1 hour. (It does just as well in shallower pans – it will rise a little.)
5 Leave to cool before turning out. Wrap in foil to store – you can keep it for a couple of weeks like that, in the fridge. It freezes well too.

The Northwest

The
Pacific Coast
& Alaska

The USA has often been called the land of rich and plenty, and nowhere is that more true than of the Pacific Coast, particularly California. Although Hawaii is referred to as the cultural 'melting pot', I find this a more accurate description of the Pacific Coast: where Hawaii has a mixture of the Polynesian and Oriental, the West Coast has this plus the Hispanic and European influences. People still move west – there is a feeling that there is more opportunity, more freedom, more hope, and of course, more sunshine! In addition, the climate is temperate – and warmer the further south you go – and the region has wonderful geographical variety. Living in San Francisco, as I did, you have the stimulus of a beautiful and cosmopolitan city, but a four-hour drive (no distance for an American motorist!) will take you to the mountains, and you can return next day to sail in the Bay. A trip southwards along the magnificent Big Sur coast will deposit you on wonderful beaches; further on is 'tinsel-town'; and beyond the Hispanic towns down by the Mexican border. A drive north will take you to the towering redwoods and the forests of Oregon; good hunting country, and some of the finest fishing waters in America.

Because of the climate, there is little that cannot be grown. The fruits and vegetables are transported all over the country and to other parts of the world, but nowhere do they taste better than here where they can be plucked and eaten ripe from the tree. A multitudinous variety of seafood is available. Most major cities like Seattle or San Francisco have their Fisherman's Wharfs, harbour areas full of wonderful restaurants, shops and stalls where the riches of the sea are displayed. It is this bounty of natural produce that forms the basis of West Coast cooking. There is really no dish that can be said to be strictly 'traditional' and the label 'typical' can only be applied to the range of ingredients, which is wide – fruits, in particular the luscious peaches and citrus fruits, and avocados; vegetables – artichokes, asparagus, and superb salad vegetables the size and quality of which astonish you; olives, nuts, grapes, and of course wines (California produces some lovely wines, in taste somewhere between the very fruity German and the dry French); not forgetting seafood.

And Alaska – no folks, we've not forgotten you but to be honest, never having lived there, I've not built up a recipe collection. However, I've consulted my friends Carol Matteson and Barbara Mitchell, who both have first-hand experience. Alaskan food seems to be similar to that of the northwestern states, with the biggest difference being in the types of meat commonly eaten. Here, caribou, elk, moose and bear hold sway. Since these aren't readily available this side of the Atlantic, we've not given recipes. These meats, bear in particular, are often minced and made into 'burgers'. These I have tasted – sometimes my father would bring back a bear from a day's hunting – and it's rather like strong beef. Alaskans love their fine seafood, and are famous for their King crab, usually simply boiled, or mixed with mayonnaise and cheese for sandwich fillings, and shrimps, boiled or pickled. They cook salmon in every possible manner – deep-fried balls (similar to Codfish balls), baked in egg custards or pies, cooked meatloaf-style, salted, or pickled as are the shrimps, used in chowders, or marinated and charcoal-grilled. As for breads, Alaskans are fond of sourdough and use it for loaves, cakes, pie crusts, even sourdough cinnamon rolls. Berries grow plentifully in the Alaskan summers so fruit pies – particularly cranberry and blueberry, and rhubarb too – feature strongly, as do relishes and ketchups, and fruit butters are quite popular too. On the whole, the food is quite simply prepared, but with such marvellous raw material, who needs to do anything more!

Cold artichoke dip

This dip will taste as good (or as bad) as the mayonnaise base, so if using bought, buy a good quality, *not* salad cream.

Makes: about 600 ml/20 fl oz.
1 × 425 g/15 oz can artichoke hearts (8-10 hearts), drained
1 × 115 g/4 oz can green chillies, chopped
115 g/4 oz Parmesan cheese, grated
8 tbsp mayonnaise

1 Chop the artichoke hearts and chillies. Mix all the ingredients and chill.
2 Turn into a serving dish or bowl, and set out crackers (it goes well with the wheat variety) or corn chips.
Serving suggestion: This also makes excellent hot canapés: put 1-2 teaspoons on melba toast and place under the grill for a minute or two, until the top begins to brown.

Smoky dip

This has a strong taste and is quite rich so you don't need much. You could use smoked oysters instead of clams. It would work, too, with smoked mussels, but this variation wouldn't be very West Coast!

Serves: 4.
1 × 100 g/3½ oz can smoked clams
85-115g/3-4 oz cream cheese
1-2 tbsp sherry
½ tsp Worcester sauce
½ tsp paprika

1 Mince or finely chop the clams.
2 Mix the cream cheese with the sherry. Add the clams, mix in the Worcester sauce and paprika. Then chill in the refrigerator.
3 Serve with wheat crackers or Melba toast.
Serving suggestion: If you would rather not use it as a dip, try it as a filling for celery 'boats' – the strong smokiness is a perfect complement to the crunchy, clean taste of celery.

Asparagus fondue fingers

A sort of up-market Welsh Rarebit – California-style! In the US it is common to use American processed cheese for this type of recipe, since it is easy to melt, but it works well with Cheddar and/or Gruyere.

Serves: 4 as a starter, or 2 as a lunch or supper dish.
450 g/1 lb cheese
1 small onion, finely minced
175 ml/6 fl oz white wine
½ tsp mustard
1 bunch asparagus (you could use frozen, or canned)
4 slices hot toast (wholemeal is best)
butter

1 Grate the cheese, and mince or very finely chop the onion.
2 Put the wine into the top of a double boiler or fondue pot. Gently heat the wine and slowly add the cheese, stirring as it melts. Add the mustard and the onion.
3 Cook the asparagus in boiling water for a few minutes until tender, and drain carefully. Melt the butter and dribble it over the spears.
4 Make the toast and cut into fingers. Place a spear on each finger, and top with the cheese sauce.

Barbecued prawns

In the States, this is known as Barbecued shrimp, but for Americans shrimp is a catch-all term. Our recipe calls for regular prawns, but you could use Pacific, King or large Mediterranean prawns.

Serves: 4.
225 g/8 oz shelled prawns
Marinade:
175 ml/6 fl oz vegetable oil
85 ml/3 fl oz sherry (dry or medium)
85 ml/3 fl oz soy sauce
2 cloves garlic, crushed
Butter sauce:
225 g/8 oz butter
juice of 1 lemon
½ tsp salt
1 tbsp Worcester sauce
1 tbsp soy sauce
3-4 dashes Tabasco sauce
2 cloves garlic, crushed

1 Thaw the prawns, if using frozen, rinse and drain.
2 Mix all the ingredients for the marinade, add the prawns and leave for 3-4 hours, in the refrigerator, turning the prawns every so often.
3 Just before you are ready to serve, lay the prawns on foil in the grill pan. Heat the grill, but do not put the prawns under it yet.
4 Make the butter sauce by melting the butter and adding all the other ingredients. Heat gently, and stir until it is well blended.
5 Place the prawns under the grill and heat through, turning once.
6 Serve the prawns on individual plates, with cocktail sticks. Serve the sauce as a side dip, or in individual bowls. Don't worry if you seem to have rather a lot of butter sauce – it disappears all the same. Our guests found it great for dunking bread. The sauce is *very* buttery, so you may find that its not to everyone's taste. For those of you who do like it, it would go well with lobster, too, or snails.

Stuffed tomatoes

Refreshing and tangy, this is a good starter or light lunch dish, which is actually more filling than it looks.

Serves: 4.
4 beefsteak tomatoes
2 × 200 g/7 oz cans tuna
1 small onion, finely sliced
6-8 tbsp mayonnaise
1 tsp black pepper
½ tsp salt
Garnish:
lettuce leaves
lemon wedges

1 Slice the tops off the tomatoes, and gently scoop out the insides, leaving a shell that is about 3 mm/¼ in thick.
2 Discarding some of the juice and pips, dice the pulp and put it into a mixing bowl.
3 Drain the tuna (and if canned in oil, rinse off as much as possible) and flake into the tomato pulp.
4 Slice the onion, and add to the tomato and tuna, along with the mayonnaise, pepper and salt. Mix all together well. Spoon into the tomatoes so that each is well filled. If you like, chill slightly before serving.
5 Serve on lettuce leaves, with a lemon wedge on each tomato.

Eggs benedict

Serves: 4.
4 eggs
350 g/12 oz Hollandaise sauce (see recipe on page 15)
4 slices back bacon
2 'English-style' muffins

6This is actually a simpler version of Eggs hussarde (see page 15). We include it because it is *the* Californian brunch, linked in Kenna's mind with warm, sunny Sundays in Tiberon, a small town across the bay from San Francisco. 9

1 Make the Hollandaise sauce and set aside, but keep warm.
2 Grill (or fry) the bacon, drain and set aside, keeping warm.
3 Poach the eggs.
4 Meanwhile, split the muffins and toast each half. Lay a slice of bacon on each, and then an egg. Cover with sauce, and serve hot.

Spinach salad

Serves: 4.
450 g/1 lb fresh spinach leaves
2-4 eggs, hardboiled
225 g/8 oz streaky bacon
Dressing:
150 ml/5 fl oz salad oil
2 tbsp white wine
2 tbsp white wine vinegar
2 tsp soy sauce
1 tsp dry mustard
1 tsp sugar
³⁄₄-1 tsp curry powder (according to taste)
1-2 cloves garlic, crushed

6Often served in West Coast restaurants (and homes too), this is a great favourite, particularly with office workers who lunch on spinach salad and bread (usually garlic bread). It is truly tasty yet simple, and makes a wonderful change from lettuce-based salads. 9

1 Hardboil the eggs.
2 Cut the bacon into smallish pieces and fry until crisp. Drain on absorbent paper.
3 Wash the spinach, drain well, and tear into smallish pieces, discarding stalks.
4 Make the dressing by adding all the ingredients together and mixing well. It's easiest to do this in a screw-top jar – just give it all a good shake.
5 Chop the eggs and put them with spinach and bacon into a salad bowl. Add the dressing, toss well and serve.
Serving suggestion: For vegetarians, omit the bacon. You can add some raw mushrooms, and possibly a handful of chopped nuts, or perhaps some sliced artichoke hearts.

Left: Barbecued prawns (recipe, page 57) and Eggs benedict

California combination salad

In this one, you can choose from the ingredients, all of which are grown in California and figure prominently on local tables. If making the salad for a lunch party, use one avocado per person, and increase all other amounts a little.

Serves: 2 as a lunch dish, or 4 as a starter.
2 ripe avocados
50 g/2 oz walnuts or 50 g/2 oz almonds (blanched)
85 g/3 oz black grapes or handful of raisins
6 asparagus spears
black or green olives (optional)
I paw-paw or papaya, sliced (optional)
palm hearts, sliced (optional)
Dressing:
2-4 tbsp lemon juice
I-2 tbsp light salad oil
I clove garlic, crushed
salt and pepper to taste
lettuce leaves to garnish

1 Halve the avocados, remove stones, peel, and chop flesh into bite-sized chunks.
2 Coarsely chop walnuts; if using almonds, sliver, or leave whole. Halve the grapes/raisins and remove seeds. If using asparagus, boil or steam till tender, and leave to cool. Slice into smaller pieces.
3 Mix your chosen ingredients together. Make the dressing and pour over the salad. Mix gently but make sure the avocado is well coated.
4 If liked, chill slightly before serving on a bed of lettuce.
Note: This will keep quite well overnight in the fridge, so long as it is covered, but any longer and the avocados will discolour.

Fruit salad

No, this isn't a mistake – fruit salad is meant to be in this section. In the States, at 'pot luck' dinners or outdoor barbecues where guests work their way along the table helping themselves to a spoonful of this and that, this is served as an accompaniment to be taken, along with other salads, with the meat. If, however, you shrink at the very thought of a whipped cream fruit salad with your barbecued chicken don't jettison it altogether – serve it as a dessert – it's wonderful!

Serves: 6-8.
Fruit *(choose 4 from list):*
I small cantaloupe or Ogen melon, balled or cubed
3 bananas, sliced into I cm/½ in pieces
I small pineapple, or equivalent canned, and well drained
115-175 g/4-6 oz seedless grapes (don't use canned – they are too mushy)
2-3 kiwi fruit, sliced
2-3 peaches, sliced
2-3 oranges
a few maraschino cherries – mostly for colour
Dressing: *(makes about 450 ml/15 fl oz)*
85-115 g/3-4 oz cream cheese, softened
2 tbsp mayonnaise
8 tbsp apricot jam
I tbsp lemon juice
½ tsp curry powder
150 ml/5 fl oz cream, whipped

1 Make the dressing: blend the cream cheese with the mayonnaise until smooth. Add the jam, lemon juice, and curry powder. Mix well and chill for I hour.
2 Whip the cream until fairly stiff, fold into dressing and chill until you are ready to serve.
3 Meanwhile prepare the fruit: slice into smallish pieces and just before you are ready to serve, fold the fruit into the dressing. Add the cherries. If serving as an accompaniment, turn out into a lettuce-lined bowl.
Note: Choose fruit in good condition. This is not the recipe for using up the over-ripe or slightly mushy. They will ruin the texture and you will have not salad but sludge. The salad is best eaten immediately; it doesn't keep well.

California swiss steak

Serves: 4.
450 g/1 lb skirt steak (or braising or stewing steak, not too thin)
50 g/2 oz flour
½-1 tsp black pepper
1 tsp salt
vegetable oil for browning meat
½ large onion (larger the better, to cut in ring slices)
1 large tomato
225 ml/8 fl oz white wine or 175 ml/6 fl oz wine, with 50 ml/2 fl oz water
½ tsp rosemary
½ tsp oregano
1 bay leaf
1 clove garlic, crushed (optional)
2-4 medium potatoes
2-4 large carrots
1 × 285 g/10½ oz can condensed cream of mushroom soup
115 g/4 oz mushrooms (optional)

1 Mix the flour with the salt and pepper, and put into a flat tin or dish. Cut the meat into 4 and lay each piece in the flour, coat, and pound, getting as much flour as possible into the meat.
2 In a large-lidded skillet, heavy-bottomed frying pan, or cast-iron casserole (large enough to take the meat in a single layer, and at least 8 cm/3 in deep), sear and brown the meat in a little oil, on a high heat.
3 Slice the onion and tomato crosswise, to get large rings. When the meat is browned, turn the heat to low, then place a slice of onion, followed by a slice of tomato on each steak, and add enough wine to come three-quarters of the way up the meat. (Do not cover the onion and tomato.) The amount will depend on the size of the pan. If you haven't enough wine, make up to required amount with water. Add the herbs, and garlic if wished, cover and cook for about 1 hour.
4 Wash but don't peel the potatoes and carrots, cut into largish chunks, and add to the pot along with the condensed soup. Stir gently, replace the lid and simmer for another ¾-1 hour. Towards the end of the time add the mushrooms. Add these whole if they are the button type, or, if larger, cut them into halves.
5 Serve hot. (This can be made in advance: it reheats well, and the taste of the wine gets stronger.)

West coast roast

Serves: as many as you wish. Choose the joint and amount of vegetables to suit your requirements.
joint of beef, for roasting (size to fit into a casserole pot)
several cloves garlic, slivered
about 450 ml/15 fl oz red wine (cooking wine)
salt and pepper
vegetables – potatoes, carrots, etc.

1 Make little slits in the meat and push the garlic slivers into the flesh. If you are using frozen meat, do this when it is still half-frozen – you'll find it much easier.
2 Season the meat by rubbing it with salt and pepper, and place in a lidded cast-iron or other casserole dish. Pour in the wine to about 5 cm/2 in depth, and, turning the joint periodically, marinate for 24 hours.
3 Heat the oven to 180°C/350°F/Gas Mark 4 and cook the joint for 2-3 hours.
4 Prepare your chosen vegetables by washing, and chopping into chunks. Add to the pot for the last hour of cooking.

Simply swordfish

> Swordfish is known as the 'steak of the sea': cut into steaks, it can be treated in much the same way as beef steak. It is rather difficult to come by here, and tends to be expensive.

Allow one swordfish steak 2.5-4 cm/1-1½ in thick per person.
1 swordfish steak per person
butter
horseradish relish

1 Heat the grill. Dot the fish steaks with butter and grill for about 7-10 minutes per side.
2 Serve hot, with horseradish relish; alternatively, serve with melted butter or melted clarified butter. A good crisp salad is all the accompaniment needed, but add a baked potato to each serving if you have hungry guests.

Spanish sole

> This is a very good recipe for a dinner party or special meal. It is a lovely combination of textures and tastes – crunchy and creamy, delicate and subtle – which perfectly complement the sole.

Serves: 4.
4 fillets of sole
Sauce:
4 spring onions, finely choped
175 g/6 oz mushrooms, chopped
150 ml/5 fl oz sherry (dry or medium)
1 tsp rosemary
½ tsp salt
150 ml/5 fl oz cream
1 tbsp butter
40-50 g/1½-2 oz almonds, slivered or flaked

1 Rinse and pat dry the fillets. Chop the spring onions and mushrooms fairly finely.
2 Pour the sherry into a frying pan and lay in the fillets in a single layer. (If your pan is not large enough, do two at a time.) Add the spring onions, mushrooms, and seasoning. Simmer on low heat for about 10 minutes.
3 Leaving the vegetables in the pan, gently remove the fish and place in a shallow heatproof dish. Heat the grill.
4 Over high heat, reduce the liquid in the frying pan by half. Lower the heat, and stir in the cream and butter. Pour the sauce over the fish and place under the grill for 4-5 minutes.
5 Sliver the almonds, and when the fish is almost done, sprinkle the nuts on top. Grill for another 1-2 minutes.
6 Serve hot, with a green salad or a vegetable such as spinach. Garlic bread is also a good accompaniment.

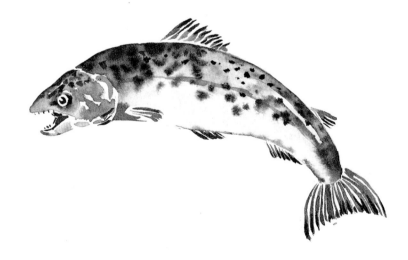

Right: Spinach salad (recipe, page 59) and Spanish sole

Halibut pimiento

'This is a dinner party dish. Halibut is a common West Coast fish and is perfect for this recipe, but you could use any firm white fish – in California they sometimes use salmon. The sauce is rich and although quite strong, it allows the taste of the fish to come through. '

Serves: 4.
4 halibut fillets
Sauce:
175 g/6 oz strong Cheddar, grated
175 g/6 oz cream cheese
1 small onion, finely chopped
4 tsp pimiento, chopped
2 tbsp fresh parsley, finely chopped
120 ml/4 fl oz white wine (dry)
1 × 285 g/10½ oz can condensed cream of tomato soup

1 Preheat the oven to 180°C/350°F/Gas Mark 4.
2 Prepare the fillets and lay in a single layer in a shallow, lightly greased baking dish.
3 Grate the cheese, prepare the onion, pimiento, and parsley. In a saucepan, combine all the sauce ingredients and cook gently on low heat, stirring until the cheese melts and the sauce is well blended. This should be quite a thick sauce, but you may need to add a little more liquid (use wine or water according to taste).
4 Pour the sauce over the fish and bake, uncovered, for 20-30 minutes or until the fish is cooked.
5 Serve hot. This delightful dish needs nothing more than a good crisp green salad as an accompaniment.

Crab artichoke casserole

'A good lunch or supper dish, this has a lovely combination of flavours – you can taste each one. Very moreish! '

Serves: 4.
225 g/8 oz crab meat (fresh or frozen is best, but you could use canned or crab sticks)
115 g/4 oz wholewheat pasta (twirls, shells, or what you will)
½ small onion, finely chopped
1 × 425 g/15 oz can artichoke hearts (8-10 hearts)
50 g/2 oz strong Cheddar, grated
50 g/2 oz butter or margarine
2 tbsp flour
1 tsp salt
½ tsp pepper
1 tsp paprika
300 ml/10 fl oz milk
1 tbsp sherry (dry or medium)

1 Preheat the oven to 180°C/350°F/Gas Mark 4. Grease a medium-sized casserole or other oven-proof dish.
2 Boil the pasta until soft (not soggy), and drain.
3 Meanwhile, flake the crab meat; slice the onion; drain and slice the artichoke hearts; and grate the cheese.
4 Melt the butter/margarine, add the flour, salt, pepper, and paprika, and stir to a smooth paste. Add the onions, and gradually stir in the milk. Bring to the boil, stirring all the while. Reduce heat to simmer for 5 minutes before adding the sherry, crab meat, artichokes, and pasta. Mix well, and turn out into the dish. Sprinkle a generous layer of cheese on top, and bake for 20 minutes.
5 Serve hot with a green salad.

Salmon alder

Serves: 4.
450 g/1 lb salmon or 4 salmon steaks
Marinade:
1 tbsp oil
2 cloves garlic
1 small onion, finely chopped
1-2 sprigs fresh parsley
1 tsp each of basil, rosemary, thyme, marjoram, oregano, tarragon
pinch of sage
50 ml/2 fl oz vermouth
50 ml/2 fl oz lemon juice
4-5 dashes Tabasco sauce
1 tbsp Worcester sauce

1 Sauté the garlic, onion and parsley in oil. When they have softened, add all the seasonings, vermouth, lemon juice, and the Tabasco and Worcester sauces. Mix well together and stir to form a marinade.
2 Pour the marinade over the salmon and marinate for 24 hours, turning the fish occasionally.
3 Wrap each piece of fish in foil, folded to seal, and cook over charcoal or bake in the oven at 180°C/350°F/Gas Mark 4 for about 15 minutes.
4 Serve hot or cold.

Sweet and sour meatballs

Makes: 18 meatballs, enough for 4 people.
450 g/1 lb good quality minced beef
1 small onion, minced
85 g/3 oz breadcrumbs
1 tsp salt
1 tsp pepper
1 egg
vegetable oil for browning
Sauce:
2 sticks celery, cut into 1 cm/½ in pieces
1 small-medium red pepper, cut into strips
1 small-medium green pepper, cut into strips
350 ml/12 fl oz water
50-85 ml/2-3 fl oz vinegar (preferably cider, but absolutely not malt)
40-50 g/1½-2 oz brown sugar
2 tbsp soy sauce
2 tsp cornflour or arrowroot
1 × 225 g/8 oz can pineapple (slices or chunks), drained

1 Make the meatballs: mince the onion, add to the meat and mix all the ingredients except the oil together. Form into balls about the size of golf balls. In a large, heavy-bottomed pan, heat oil no more than 1 cm/½ in deep, and brown the meatballs, turning gently every so often.
2 Prepare the vegetables for the sauce. When the meatballs are browned, remove them from the pan and set aside. In the same oil, gently sauté the vegetables for about 5 minutes.
3 Mix the water, vinegar, sugar and soy sauce in a bowl. Stir 2 tablespoons cold water into the cornflour and add to the sauce. Now pour the sauce on to the vegetables, stir, and cook for 3 minutes.
4 Return the meatballs to the pan, and heat gently for a few minutes until the balls have heated through in the sauce.
5 Drain the pineapple and add. Serve hot, on boiled rice, or noodles.
Note: If you want to prepare the dish in advance, cook up to the point of adding the pineapple. Add the fruit when you reheat to serve.

'As you wish' wok pot

❝A wonderful way to turn some leftovers into a tasty meal.❞

Serves: 4.
about 450 g/1 lb beef or pork, cut into strips
or 3 good-sized chicken pieces, skinned, boned and cut into strips
or 225 g/8 oz shelled prawns
sesame oil for coating wok
light vegetable or peanut (groundnut) oil for frying
Marinade:
teriyaki sauce, to cover meat or seafood (use commercially made) or Korean barbecue sauce (see page 80)
Vegetables *(choose 3 or 4 from the following):*
mushrooms, sliced
spring onions, chopped
Chinese leaves, shredded or chopped
mangetout (snow peas)
cabbage, white or green, shredded
asparagus (fresh not canned)
broccoli, broken into florets
cauliflower, broken into florets
water chestnuts
bamboo shoots

1 Prepare the meat or seafood, place in a shallow dish, and cover with teriyaki sauce.
Note: It tastes best if you can allow the meat/seafood to marinate for a couple of hours, but if you haven't the time, it still tastes pretty good.
2 Prepare the vegetables. Using a paper towel, lightly coat the wok with a thin layer of sesame oil. This lends a subtle and slightly nutty flavour.
3 Pour a small amount of vegetable oil into the wok and heat on high. With a slotted spoon remove the meat from the marinade, and cook until almost done (4-5 minutes). Return the meat to the marinade.
4 If necessary add a little more oil to the wok and cook the vegetables for 2-3 minutes. Add the meat, with the marinade, stir into the vegetables and cover with the steamer lid for 2 minutes or so, to finish off. Don't overcook – the vegetables should be just tender.
5 Serve immediately, with rice, boiled or fried (see recipe on page 84), or with noodles, or just as it is. As a condiment you may like to serve teriyaki or soy sauce.
Serving suggestion: If you like, toss in a handful of nuts – cashews taste particularly good.

Oregon wild rice with filberts

❝Wild rice is not actually rice but the seed of an aquatic grass, and was first harvested by the American Indians. Here, it is extremely expensive and quite difficult to find. It has a slightly nutty flavour and is delicious used on its own or mixed in with rice. Filberts are what we know as hazel or cob nuts. This goes well with game.❞

Serves: 4 as a main dish, or 6-8 as a side dish.
175-225 g/6-8 oz wild rice, washed and drained
3-4 sticks celery, chopped
115 g/4 oz mushrooms, sliced
2 small onions, chopped
50 g/2 oz butter
85-115 g/3-4 oz hazelnuts
½ tsp salt
½ tsp black pepper
½ tsp sage
450 ml/15 fl oz chicken stock (preferably homemade, but a cube will suffice)

1 Cover the washed and drained wild rice with boiling water, and leave standing for 15-20 minutes, then drain and set aside.
2 Prepare the vegetables. Heat the butter in a frying pan and sauté the nuts for a few minutes. Remove the nuts and set aside. Sauté the vegetables until tender.
3 If using a stock cube, make it up now. Add the stock to the vegetables, with the seasoning (watch the salt, if using a cube). Add the drained wild rice and bring to the boil. Reduce the heat and simmer, covered, for 35-45 minutes, until the liquid is absorbed. The grains should be beginning to open.
4 Stir in the nuts, allowing them a minute or two to heat through. Adjust the seasoning, and serve.

Right: 'As you wish' wok pot

Hollywood dessert

❝Oh, this is *so* good. To describe it as a fruit pie seems both inaccurate and inadequate. In fact, you hardly notice the fruit (but don't omit); it creates a moist texture at the bottom of the pie, the sugar melts down through the batter, turning it all a rich brown, and the top bakes to a dark crunchy crust. ❞

115 g/4 oz plain white flour
½ tsp bicarbonate of soda
½ tsp salt
225 g/8 oz white sugar (granulated or caster)
I egg
I × 400 g/14 oz can fruit cocktail, drained
115 g/4 oz soft light or dark brown sugar (not demerara)
50-85 g/2-3 oz walnuts, coarsely chopped

1 Preheat the oven to 150°C/300°F/Gas Mark 2, and lightly grease a 23 cm/9 in ovenproof pie dish or flan tin.
2 Sift the flour, soda and salt into a bowl and mix in the white sugar.
3 Beat the egg and add to the mixture. Drain the fruit cocktail, and mix in. Turn out into the greased pie dish.
4 Put a thickish layer of brown sugar over the top, and add a generous sprinkling of coarsely chopped walnuts.
5 Bake for about I hour. Serve warm with whipped cream.
Note: You could use almost any sort of canned fruit for this recipe – peaches would be good. You can use fresh fruit, in which case, I think it better to stew it gently first, and drain well. Avoid fruits that 'bleed'.

Almond peaches

❝A lot of peaches are grown in Washington State, and this combines the best of home produce with the characteristic lightness of style. Impressive, but actually very simple, this is the ideal dessert to serve after a heavy meal. ❞

Serves: 4.
4 peaches (8 halves), fresh or canned
50 g/2 oz almond nibs, lightly toasted
I tsp grated orange peel
2 tbsp icing sugar
120 ml/4 fl oz medium sherry

1 Preheat the oven to 180°C/350°F/Gas Mark 4.
2 If using fresh peaches, peel and halve. If using canned, drain well. Lay halves in a single layer in a shallow ovenproof dish.
3 Lightly toast the almond nibs, grate the peel, and mix both with the icing sugar. Spoon the mixture into the peach halves.
4 Gently dribble the sherry over the peaches, letting it soak into each half. If you have any remaining, just pour into the dish. Bake uncovered for 20-30 minutes.
5 Serve hot or cold. This really needs no addition, but if you prefer, you could serve it with a dollop of cream whipped up with a few drops of almond essence. It goes well with ratafia biscuits or *langues de chats*.

San Francisco sourdough bread

Makes: 1 large loaf.
Starter:
1 medium-large potato
450 g/1 lb strong white flour
up to 900 ml/30 fl oz water
225 g/8 oz sugar
Bread:
2 tsp dried yeast
350 ml/12 fl oz water or 175 ml/6 fl oz water, with 175 ml/6 fl oz beer
675-900 g/1½-2 lb strong white flour
2 tsp salt

6This is a lovely bread, pale golden on top, quite thick in texture, with, as the name indicates, a slightly sour taste. It's enormously popular in San Francisco, and departing travellers often take loaves with them. 9

1 Make the starter: boil the potato, reserving liquid. Peel and mash thoroughly.
2 Add enough tepid water to the potato water to make 900 ml/30 fl oz, and stir into the mashed potato. Add flour and sugar to make a thick batter. Cover the bowl with clingfilm, and then with a towel or blanket, and place in a warm, draughtless nook (an airing cupboard is ideal) for about 36 hours. It is difficult to be exact – you want to catch the starter when it has a very strong smell something like a sour wood varnish. This can take 24-48 hours. Too little time and you won't have a sourdough at all, too long and it will be past its best and the sour taste will be diminished. The starter is designed to be kept going – if you feel you'd rather not start a bakery, reduce the starter ingredients by half, and use it all at once.
3 Make the bread: empty 225 g/8 oz of the starter into a mixing bowl. (If you want to keep it going, add to the remainder another 225 g/8 oz flour and 225 ml/8 fl oz water, cover again, and return to a warm place for another 24-48 hours, so that it will be ready for the next batch.)
4 Dissolve the yeast in water or water/beer mix, and add to the starter.
5 Mix in the flour and salt to form a soft dough. Knead for 10-15 minutes until the dough is smooth and elastic. Place in a lightly oiled bowl to rise to about double in size (about 2 hours). Knock down, knead and shape into a round or oval. Leave to prove – about another 1½ hours. You should now have a large smooth disc. While it is proving, heat the oven to 190°C/375°F/Gas Mark 5.
6 Bake at 190°C/375°F/Gas Mark 5 for 15 minutes, reduce heat to 180°C/350°F/Gas Mark 4 and bake another 20 minutes, then turn down to 110°C/225°F/Gas Mark ½ for the final 15-25 minutes.
Note: You can, of course, make this amount into 2 smaller loaves. It freezes very well.

Apple butter

Fills 2 × 300 ml/10 fl oz jars. If you wish to make more, increase ingredients in proportion to the amount of apples.
900 g/2 lb eating apples
225 ml/8-12 fl oz water
about 225 g/8 oz granulated sugar
2 tsp cinnamon
1 tsp cloves
¼ tsp allspice

6Fruit butters were at one time commonly found in this country but seem now to have passed out of favour, along with so many of the older methods of preserving food. Fruit butters are rather like jam in which the fruit has been puréed – similar to other preserves such as damson 'cheese'. 9

1 Peel and quarter and apples, removing the core.
2 Put apples and water in a pan, and simmer the fruit slowly until very soft.
3 Drain fruit, and push through a sieve. (This is why the apples should be soft. At our first attempt, we undercooked them and couldn't get them through the sieve!)
4 Measure the amount and return to the pan, adding 115 g/4 oz sugar for every 225 g/8 oz of puréed apple. Add the spices.
5 Bring to a slow boil and simmer until the mixture becomes very thick (about 10-15 minutes). Consistency test: drop a small amount on to a plate. If no liquid forms around it, your mixture is thick enough.
6 Pour into hot sterilized jars, and store as you would jam.

Overleaf: Almond peaches
(recipe, page 58)

4.

Hawaii

Tropical
Island Fare

Aloha and welcome to America's tropical paradise. Four hours by air from the mainland and you're in a totally different world. The climate is always warm and sunny (even when it rains) and so are the people. Whether you arrive by plane or cruise ship you will be greeted with a hug and a lei (the traditional garland of flowers) to wear around your neck, but wherever you're from you'll be referred to as a haole *(foreigner).*

The Hawaiian Islands are referred to as the 'melting pot' of the Americas because of the wide racial mix. There are still pure Hawaiians but they are now a minority. The largest ethnic groups are the Caucasians, Chinese, Japanese, Portuguese and Koreans, but intermarriage is common, and many islanders may be a mixture of all of these! Racial background and makeup are important in terms of personal identity, and people, when introduced, will explain their own racial mix.

Of the seven main islands, the most densely populated is Oahu. It is by no means the largest but it has Honolulu, Waikiki Beach, and Pearl Harbour, so it is the main tourist centre, and in addition to the native islanders you will come across large numbers of holidaymakers, honeymooners and servicemen.

As Hawaii has a tropical climate, the food grown there is quite different from that in the rest of America, and because it is separated from the mainland by about 2000 miles, the cost of many things considered standard there is very much higher in Hawaii. Consequently, the diet centres on the locally grown food – pineapple, coconut, sugar cane, papayas, mangoes and guavas are far more common than the orchard fruits, and their use in almost all dishes, with or without meat, makes this diet somewhat sweeter than that of other regions. Pork is the main meat, and of course, seafood is abundant. The Orient exercises a gentle influence over many of the dishes, particularly in the choice of seasoning and cooking style, and it is this (perhaps to British tastes somewhat strange) combination of Oriental style with rather more tropical produce which makes the food of this region so interesting.

You can't discuss food in Hawaii without mention of a luau. A luau (pronounced 'loo-ow') is a banquet, very informal, very friendly, which centres on a pig traditionally baked on hot coals in a pit dug in the earth, though these days it is as likely to be roasted on a spit. The baking of the pig goes on through the night, with the cooks sitting up to baste the carcass while their companions sing and dance the hours away. All the food is laid out at once, on leaves or a cloth on the ground, or on a huge table. Everyone eats with their fingers, using large flat taro leaves for plates. The summer I lived in Honolulu I went for a drive with some friends around the island

on the fourth of July – Independence Day. We stopped to take in the view; there was a family luau laid out on the ground. We were instantly drawn into the festivities and left, very full, some three hours later (one hour of which was spent hugging everyone goodbye!) with such smiles on our faces.

We have not included many traditional luau dishes because of the unavailability of the ingredients: for example, 'poi' is a staple, eaten as is rice or potatoes. It has a bland taste – to foreigners unfamiliar and generally unappreciated – and we've not found any in London yet!

Pigeon English – a mixture of English and Hawaiian – is commonly used among the natives. So, pour yourself a Mai Tai, bake a Hawaiian feast, and impress your friends with your knowledge of local customs. Begin with a toast, Okole Maluna ('Bottoms up'), wish them hauoli (joy) and a nui nui ona kaai (big appetite).

Hawaii

Char siu

> ‘Tender and juicy, this is sliced barbecued pork, Chinese style. Peanut sauce (see recipe below) is perfect with it. ’

Serves: 6.
900 g/2 lb pork, preferably a boneless roasting joint
Marinade:
120 ml/4 fl oz soy sauce
50-85 ml/2-3 fl oz sherry
I tsp cochineal or red food colouring
2 cloves garlic, crushed
1-2 tsp ground ginger or freshly grated ginger root, in which case use less
4-6 tbsp honey

1 Mix together all the ingredients for the marinade. Pour into a shallow dish large enough to hold the meat in a single layer.
2 Cut the pork lengthwise into, say, 3 equal pieces, and lay in the marinade, cover and leave in the refrigerator for 12-24 hours. Remember to turn the meat now and then.
3 Remove the meat from the marinade and discard the juice. Place the meat on a rack set in a shallow pan with 1-2.5 cm/½-1 in water. Bake at 170°C/325°F/Gas Mark 3 for about 30 minutes.
4 Remove the pan from the oven and allow the meat to cool. With a very sharp knife slice the meat very thinly. Serve the cooked pork as it is, or with a savory sauce such as Peanut sauce (see recipe below).

Peanut sauce

> ‘This is a rather thick sauce, best served warm. It also makes a tasty baste for barbecued pork or chicken. ’

Makes: about 600 ml/20 fl oz.
8 oz peanuts, ground
I medium onion, chopped
2-3 cloves garlic, chopped
2.5 cm/I in piece ginger root, chopped
½ tsp chilli powder
1½ tsp lemon juice
450-600 ml/15-20 fl oz water
2 tbsp oil
I tsp sugar
2 tsp salt

1 Chop the onion, garlic and ginger, and place in a blender with the chilli powder.
2 Add the lemon juice to the water and pour a little into the blender. Whizz for a few seconds until you have a smooth purée.
3 Pour the oil into a wok or frying pan and heat. Add the onion purée and cook, stirring, for 4-5 minutes, until much of the moisture has been cooked off. Turn the heat to medium-low.
4 Gradually add the rest of the liquid, stirring until it is well mixed.
5 Add the ground peanuts, sugar, and salt. Stir gently until you have a thickish sauce. Cook for another 4-5 minutes.
6 Serve warm. If you have made the sauce in advance you may find that it has become too thick – loosen by adding a little milk, and warm through over gentle heat.

Overleaf: Pupu skewers (recipe, page 77) and Coconut coleslaw (recipe, page 81)

Shrimp tempura

Serves: 4.
350 g/12 oz unshelled prawns
vegetable oil for deep frying
apricot sauce (see recipe below)
soy sauce
Batter:
50-85 g/2-3 oz cornflour
50 g/2 oz plain white flour
½ tsp salt
I egg
120 ml/4 fl oz water

1 Allow the prawns to thaw. If using Pacific prawns, split along back and open to form butterflies. Rinse and drain well. If using apricot sauce, make it now.
2 Make the batter: whisk together all the ingredients in a bowl.
3 Pour the oil into a frying pan to a depth of 2.5 cm/1 in. Heat through well.
4 Dip the prawns one by one into the batter and drop into the hot oil. When the prawn bobs to the surface, turn it over and cook until light golden. Remove with a slotted spoon and drain on absorbent paper.
5 Serve on individual plates, with a small pot of apricot sauce and another of soy sauce for each person. Dip prawns into sauces and eat with your fingers!

Apricot sauce

6This sauce is particularly tasty with Shrimp tempura. 9

Makes: about 600 ml/20 fl oz.
115 g/4 oz dried apricots (Hunza have the best flavour)
225 ml/8 fl oz water
2 tbsp sugar
pinch of salt
I tsp paprika
50 ml/2 fl oz white rum
2 tbsp cider vinegar
2 tbsp honey or apricot jam

1 Soak the apricots in water, cook until soft, and remove the stones. Drain.
2 Blend the apricots and other ingredients until you have a smooth purée. Serve slightly warm.

Pupu skewers

6*Pupu* is the Hawaiian word for *hors d'oeuvres* – these barbecued skewers are designed as appetizers, to be served as part of a large spread. 9

Makes: about 15 small skewers.
450 g/1 lb piece of ham, cubed
225 g/8 oz streaky bacon
450 g/1 lb pineapple cubes, fresh or canned, drained
50-115 g/2-4 oz stuffed green olives
15 cherry tomatoes or 4 salad tomatoes, quartered
15 small onions
Marinade:
3 tbsp soy sauce
1½ tbsp honey
1½ tbsp sherry
½ tsp grated orange peel
I clove garlic, crushed

1 Cut the ham into cubes. Mix the marinade and soak the ham for several hours or overnight.
2 Cut the bacon slices in half. Peel the onions. Drain the pineapple and wrap each cube in a piece of bacon. Thread on to a skewer. Add an olive, a cube of ham, a tomato, an onion, another bacon-wrapped pineapple cube and another olive. Grill for about 5 minutes turning once or twice. Best served hot.

H a w a i i

Hawaiian pork chops

‘An easy and delicious way to serve chops. ’

Serves: 4-6.
6 pork chops (or pork steaks), 2.5 cm/1 in thick, trimmed of fat
1 tbsp vegetable oil
450 g/1 lb can of pineapple rings, with juice
85 ml/3 fl oz soy sauce
2.5 cm/1 in freshly grated ginger root
2 cloves garlic, crushed
1 large spring onion, finely chopped
2 tbsp cornflour mixed to a paste with 1 tbsp water

1 In a frying pan, brown the pork chops slowly in oil.
2 Meanwhile, drain the pineapple, reserving the juice. To this juice add the soy sauce, ginger and garlic, and the chopped spring onion.
3 Remove the chops from the pan, and drain off the fat. Pour the soy mixture into the pan, add the cornflour paste and stir until you have a thick gravy.
4 Add the pork chops and simmer on low for 45 minutes, turning the meat once or twice so it is well covered.
5 Towards the end of the 45 minute cooking time, add the drained pineapple rings – just arrange them carefully on top of each chop – and cook the chops for a further 10 minutes, allowing the fruit to warm through.
6 Serve hot; noodles are a good accompaniment.

Island ribs

‘A pleasant alternative to the more usual spicy spare ribs – this gives a sharper taste. Quite easy to do, but you need to keep watch while the ribs cook. ’

Serves: 4-6.
1.75 kg/4 lb pork ribs (try to get uncut racks)
Glaze:
115 g/4 oz (8 tbsp) molasses
8 tbsp tomato ketchup
1 bunch spring onions, finely chopped
2 tbsp soy sauce
1 tbsp grated lemon peel
juice of 1 lemon
1 tsp dry mustard powder
½ tsp black pepper
3 cloves garlic, crushed
2 cloves, whole
1 tbsp butter

1 Place the racks of ribs in a large shallow baking pan, and cook, uncovered, in the oven for 45 minutes at 170°C/325°F/Gas Mark 3.
2 Meanwhile, put all the ingredients for the glaze into a saucepan, bring to the boil, and remove from the heat. Remove the ribs from the oven, drain off the fat, and pour the glaze over the ribs.
3 Return to the oven for another 45 minutes, basting every 15 minutes or so, and turning the ribs now and then.
4 Serve hot.
Note: You can, of course, cook the ribs over charcoal – it adds a certain something!

Right: Island ribs

H a w a i i

Korean bul kokee

'This is a good easy one to serve for guests, or the family. The sauce has quite a strong flavour, and it may be used in place of teriyaki sauce, in any recipe calling for the latter. It can be kept in the fridge, in a screw-top jar. '

Serves: 4.
450 g/1 lb meat (use topside or skirt)
Barbecue sauce:
4 tsp soy sauce
50 ml/2 fl oz water
1 tbsp sesame oil
2-3 dashes Tabasco sauce
2 tbsp sugar
2-3 cloves garlic, crushed
2.5 cm/1 in piece ginger root, grated
1 tbsp sesame seeds, toasted and ground
1 tsp black pepper
1-2 spring onions, finely chopped

1 Mix all the sauce ingredients together as a marinade.
2 Slice the meat into thin strips 4×8 cm/1½×3 in and place in the marinade. Leave for at least 1 hour.
3 Heat the grill. Spread the strips of meat on the pan, and grill, turning once.
4 While the meat is cooking, gently heat the marinade.
5 Serve hot over boiled white rice, using the marinade as gravy.
Note: This is a tasty way with ribs. Using the above sauce, let the ribs (or other meat) marinate overnight, and barbecue, preferably over coals.

Chicken with peanuts

'This is very simple to do – and it looks good too! It's not a 'hot' dish, unless you happen to swallow a pepper – if you prefer, remove them before serving. '

Serves: 4.
3 large chicken breasts, uncooked
175 ml/6 fl oz water
115 g/4 oz peanuts, shelled and roasted, not salted
2 tbsp oil
2 cloves garlic, crushed
3-4 hot dried red peppers
1 bunch spring onions, chopped (use all the onions – tops too!)
2 tbsp soy sauce
½ tbsp cornflour mixed with 1½ tbsp water
¼ tsp white sugar
2 tbsp sherry

1 Remove the skin from the chicken, cut the meat from the bone, and dice. Place the skin and bones in a pan with the water, and simmer for stock.
2 Rub the brown skins off the peanuts. Toast the nuts under the grill, until golden brown.
3 In a frying pan, skillet, or cast-iron casserole dish, heat the oil, add the meat, and garlic, and sauté for about 5 minutes.
4 Add the hot peppers, spring onions, peanuts, and the soy sauce.
5 Mix the cornflour with water. Strain the stock and pour it into the meat. When the mixture boils add the cornflour paste, sugar and the sherry. Stir to mix well, cover and cook for a few minutes until it thickens.
6 Serve with plain boiled rice, and if you like, some Chinese vegetables.

Crab rice salad bowl

Too often rice salads are rice plus bits. This is everything else plus a little rice, and all the tastier for that. A lovely combination of textures – crunchy, juicy, light and refreshing – this is one that really comes into its own on a hot summer day.

Serves: 4 for a light lunch or supper, or 8 as a side dish.
450 g/1 lb crab meat
85-115 g/3-4 oz long-grain white rice
3 large tomatoes
1 small can water chestnuts
½ small green pepper
50 g/2 oz blanched almonds, chopped
Dressing:
4 tbsp mayonnaise
2 tbsp tarragon vinegar
½ tsp oregano
1 tsp salt

1 Boil the long-grain white rice, drain and leave to cool.
2 Flake the crab meat into a mixing bowl.
3 Chop the tomatoes, water chestnuts, pepper and almonds, and add to the crab meat. Add the rice and mix well.
4 Make the dressing: add all the ingredients, mix and pour over the salad, stirring in. Chill.
5 Serve on lettuce leaves, or in a lettuce-lined bowl.

Coconut coleslaw

A very unusual coleslaw this, and on the sweetish side. It's a good party dish and goes well with ham or barbecued skewers.

Serves: 6-8 as a side dish.
¼ cabbage head, white or green, shredded
1 small can pineapple chunks or cubes, drained
115 g/4 oz dates, stoned and chopped
50 g/2 oz desiccated coconut
toasted almonds for garnish
Dressing:
50 ml/2 fl oz sour cream
3 tsp honey
2 tsp lemon juice
½ tsp ground ginger

1 Shred the cabbage into a bowl. Drain and roughly chop the pineapple and add. Chop the dates and mix in along with the coconut.
2 Mix together the dressing ingredients, pour over the coleslaw, and mix well. Chill before serving. Sprinkle with almonds.

Polynesian chicken salad

'A simple and very refreshing salad for hot weather. '

Serves: 4.
4 good-sized chicken pieces, cooked, skinned, boned and cut into small pieces
4-5 sticks celery, diced or chopped
115 g/4 oz seedless grapes
2 large carrots, coarsely grated
50-85 g/2-3 oz almonds, blanched, halved, and toasted lightly
1 small can pineapple cubes, drained or fresh pineapple, cubed (optional)
175 g/6 oz mayonnaise
85 ml/3 fl oz sour cream
1½ tsp lemon juice
1-2 tsp curry powder, to taste
½-1 tsp salt, to taste
lettuce leaves to garnish

1 Prepare the chicken, and leave to cool. Chop and grate the vegetables. Halve and toast the almonds. Put all into a large mixing bowl. Add pineapple, if wished.
2 Mix together the mayonnaise, sour cream, lemon juice and season to taste. (If you like, you can simply put all the ingredients into the same bowl and mix together. There is no real need to mix the dressing separately first, unless you are nervous of the seasoning and prefer to test it in advance.)
3 Mix all together, chill, and serve on a bed of lettuce leaves or in a lettuce-lined bowl.

Miko miko spinach

'*Miko miko* means 'tasty' and this certainly is. A really unusual way with spinach, this has a delicious but not too sweet, coconutty taste, which doesn't overpower the spinach. '

Serves: 4 as a vegetable side dish.
225 g/8 oz fresh spinach leaves, stripped from stalks (about 450 g/1 lb in total)
225 g/8 oz cottage cheese
85-115 g/3-4 oz desiccated coconut
2 eggs
150 ml/5 fl oz sour cream
3 tbsp flour
2 tbsp soy sauce

1 Preheat the oven to 180°C/350°F/Gas Mark 4. Grease a shallow casserole or ovenproof dish.
2 Strip the spinach leaves from the stalks, wash and drain well. Chop fairly finely.
3 Mix the cottage cheese with the desiccated coconut and add to the spinach, mixing all in well.
4 Beat together the eggs, 25 ml/1 fl oz sour cream, 2 tablespoons flour, and 1 tablespoon soy sauce until smooth. (You may find it easier to do this in a blender.) Stir this into the spinach and turn out into the casserole dish.
5 Beat the remaining sour cream with 1 tablespoon flour and 1 tablespoon soy sauce, and spread on top of the spinach. Bake for about 30 minutes. When cooked, leave it standing (out of the oven) for 5 minutes or so, before serving.
Note: Although this is a vegetable side dish, we would happily serve it as a light lunch or supper, accompanied by nothing grander than a good tomato salad.

Right: Polynesian chicken salad

Hawaii

Gingered carrots

‘A common way of cooking carrots as an accompaniment to almost any Hawaiian main course. ’

Serves: 4.
4 large carrots, sliced diagonally in pieces 5 mm/¼ in thick
120 ml/4 fl oz orange juice
50 ml/2 fl oz chicken stock (if not using fresh, use about ¼ cube with water)
2 whole cloves
2.5 cm/1 in cube ginger root, freshly grated
grated rind of ½ lemon
1½ tbsp brown sugar

1 Chop the carrots and place in a saucepan with all the other ingredients except the sugar. Bring to the boil.
2 Reduce the heat, stir in the sugar, cover and simmer until carrots are tender – it takes about 30 minutes, but may vary a little either way.

Fried rice

‘An essential accompaniment to oriental-style dishes. ’

Serves: 4.
175-225 g/6-8 oz white long grain rice
1 bunch spring onions, chopped
4 tbsp vegetable oil
2 tbsp soy sauce
2 eggs

1 Boil the white long grain rice, and then drain.
2 Chop the spring onions.
3 Heat the oil in a wok, on high heat (you could use a frying pan). Add the rice and onions, and the soy sauce, and stir and turn so as not to burn (though no matter if you do – it rather adds to the flavour). Cook for about 4-5 minutes.
4 Make a well in the centre, break in the eggs, breaking the yolks. Let them cook until almost set, and then, with a fork, mix the egg in well with the rice. Serve hot.
Note: We give dry weight for the rice – you can use leftover boiled rice.

Haupia (*Luau coconut pudding*)

❛Pronounced 'How-pee-ah', this is traditionally served at luaus. It is sweet and strongly coconutty, with a texture akin to a rather solid blancmange. If you have a sweet tooth you may find it an interesting and unusual addition to your repertoire. ❜

Serves: about 12. It's eaten in small cubes.
150 g/5 oz creamed coconut (in a block)
350 ml/12 fl oz hot water
6 tbsp white sugar
6 tbsp arrowroot or cornflour
dash of salt
225 ml/8 fl oz milk

1 Grate or break the creamed coconut into small pieces, and mix with the hot (not boiling) water, mashing and stirring until the mixture makes a smooth, creamy milk. (You could use a blender.)
2 In another bowl, put the sugar, arrowroot and salt, and mix with half the coconut milk.
3 In a saucepan, mix the remaining coconut milk with the milk. Heat, gently stirring all the while, and gradually add the arrowroot mixture. Keep stirring until it thickens. This happens rather suddenly, so beware.
4 Pour into a fairly shallow pan or dish (a 900 g/2 lb loaf tin will do) – the mixture should lie about 5 cm/2 in deep. Smooth the top and chill.
5 Cut into squares to serve.

Hawaiian lemon bread

❛In the States this would be served as a dessert, as a cake with morning coffee, or even, says Kenna, for breakfast! Here we would probably class it as a cake, and happily serve it for elevenses or afternoon tea. It has a good strong taste of the fruit and a slightly crunchy glaze. ❜

50 g/2 oz butter or margarine
175 g/6 oz white sugar
2 eggs, lightly beaten
grated rind of 1 lemon
225 g/8 oz plain white flour
2½ tsp baking powder
1 tsp salt
175 ml/6 fl oz milk
50-85 g/2-3 oz walnuts, chopped
Glaze:
1 tbsp lemon juice
2 tbsp white sugar

1 Preheat the oven to 180°C/350°F/Gas Mark 4 (or 170°C/325°F/Gas Mark 3 if you are using a glass baking dish). Grease a 900 g/2 lb ovenproof dish or loaf tin.
2 In a mixing bowl, cream together the butter/margarine and the sugar. Add the beaten eggs and mix in, along with the grated lemon rind.
3 Sift together the flour, baking powder and salt, and add a little to the creamed mixture. Next add some of the milk and, alternating, add the remaining flour and milk, mixing until the ingredients are well blended.
4 Chop the nuts and stir into the mixture. Turn out into the greased ovenproof dish or loaf tin, and bake for about 1 hour.
5 Prepare the glaze: mix together the lemon juice and sugar. When the lemon bread is cooked, remove from the oven. Let it stand for a minute or two before pouring the glaze over the hot loaf. Leave to cool before serving.

Hawaii

Pineapple cream dreamboats

'These are delicious, but rich. One boat is really a very large single helping – if you are on food-sharing terms, serve one between two, otherwise cut the pineapple into thickish rings and serve 4, piling the cream filling into the ring centres. '

Serves: 2-4.
1 fresh pineapple
150 ml/5 fl oz natural yoghurt
150 ml/5 fl oz double cream
2 tsp lemon juice
1-2 tsp honey
50 g/2 oz grated creamed coconut (optional)
2 egg whites

1 Slice the pineapple in half lengthwise, cutting through the leaves so they remain attached. Scoop out the flesh and reserve with as much juice as possible. Allow the 'boats' to drain, and then place in the refrigerator to chill.
2 Crush the pineapple flesh, reserving the juice.
3 In a bowl, mix the yoghurt, double cream, lemon juice, and up to 85 ml/3 fl oz of the reserved pineapple juice, and the honey. Grate the creamed coconut into the mixture. Add the pineapple flesh and mix well. If you prefer, use an electric whisk, and beat until it is well blended, thick and creamy.
4 Pour into a container, cover and place in the freezer or icebox for about 3 hours. Remove, and beat until smooth.
5 Beat the egg whites until stiff. Fold in the pineapple mixture gently, and pour into the container. Return to the ice box for several hours.
6 Remove an hour or so before you are ready to serve – the mixture should be softly scoopable but not runny. Spoon into the chilled 'boats', piling high, and serve.
Serving suggestion: The filling can be made with canned pineapple (1 × 225 g/8 oz can, unsweetened juice) and served in sundae dishes or glasses.

Right: Pineapple cream dreamboats

5.

The Midwest

*A*nd now home (for me anyway) to the Midwest – the heart of the nation – thousands of square miles of farmlands on which are produced the staples for the rest of the States, and overseas too. The long and monotonous drive from Milwaukee, Wisconsin to Denver, Colorado – 1400 miles – takes you through the Wisconsin dairy farms, the Iowan cornfields, and the wheatfields of Nebraska; areas which provide much of the wealth of the nation.

The climate varies a bit from Ohio to Montana, but the winters are cold and the four seasons clearly defined. It is in that way similar to the climate of Northern Europe and has been settled mainly by Scandinavians, Germans, and Slavs, many of whom are still only first or second generation newcomers. City areas reflect the differing nationalities, each with their own churches and halls, their own butchers and bakers too. Links with 'the old country' are still strong and there is no problem in finding someone to translate letters, though this is likely to die out soon. My teen-age children, in common with many of their age, have no interest, at least yet, in their roots.

The older Midwesterners, particularly those outside the large cities, are hard-working and proud people from European farming stock, who would rather eat cat-food than collect unemployment benefits. Life may be hard but such independence is encouraged. Religion is still strong – states like Kansas and Nebraska are considered part of 'the Bible belt' – and so are family ties. Weddings, funerals, and holy days are times of great family reunions. Food is a focal point of all such events, and the spread is likely to be incredible! It is part of the fabric of this society; to go visiting or to receive guests, however informally, without food being laid on the table, is unthinkable.

The diet tends to be 'peasant' food (I don't say that offensively): it is basic, warming, comforting, and nourishing, stemming, as it does, from the needs of a community involved in hard physical outdoor work and now, in the cities, heavy industrial work. Meat and potatoes are the mainstay, and the style has Northern-European influences but, as we noted with Mexican food in the Southwest, it has been 'Americanized'. When I lived in Munich, I searched for a recipe for German potato salad that I remembered as a child, but I never found one until I returned to visit my family in Milwaukee. This city in particular has a strong German background and, perhaps because of it, is known as the Beer City of the States, for all the lager they brew.

Chicago has now a vast mix of races, among them a strong Irish contingent. A few years back, the city had Mayor Daly, who came from Irish stock, and every year on St Patrick's Day, Chicago's river was dyed green!

You will find that many of the recipes in this section are of Slavic origin. All four of my grandparents were immigrants from north-western Yugoslavia, and my maternal grandmother lived with us during the time my brothers and I were growing up. She spent all day in the kitchen, and there were always lots of cakes and home-made sweets waiting for us when we came home from school. When my parents arrived from work we all sat down to dinner – a huge meal of several main courses and side dishes. There was always the new dish of the day, plus the leftovers from preceding dinners, until all was eaten. It's no wonder I was overweight until I moved away from home – and my grandmother called me skinny!

So, when you've had a hard day, when it's freezing outside, or when you need to feed hungry mouths and you don't have to be fancy or produce a gourmet meal, turn to this section. It's not always very stunning to look at, and it tends to be low on seasoning and consequently fairly bland, but it will put fire in your belly and warm the cockles of your heart!

Brown flour soup

'Also known as Ein Pren, this is a heartier peasant version of Egg drop soup, with a surprisingly delicate taste. '

Serves: 4-6.
2 tbsp lard or vegetable shortening
2 tbsp plain white flour
2 cloves garlic, crushed
1 tsp paprika
2 tsp salt
1 tsp black pepper
1-1.5 l/35-40 fl oz boiling water
3 eggs, lightly beaten

1 Melt the lard/shortening in a saucepan, and add the flour. Stirring constantly, cook until it browns (be careful not to let it burn). Keep the heat low. After 20-30 minutes it will suddenly give off a wonderful nutty aroma, and turn a gingery brown. (It is essential to brown the flour properly for the nuttiness to be present.)
2 Set the water to boil. Remove the roux from the heat, add the garlic and paprika, and salt. Keep stirring and gradually add the boiling water. Stir until well mixed, return to a low heat and leave to simmer, uncovered, for about 30 minutes.
3 Lightly beat the eggs. Remove the soup from the heat, very gently pour in eggs, stir once or twice, but allow the eggs to form curds.
4 Serve hot with lashings of black pepper.

Bean soup with dumplings

'Another winter warmer – it's heavy, and fairly bland, but oh so comforting! '

Serves: 4.
175-225 g/6-8 oz haricot beans (dry weight), soaked overnight
1.7 l/60 fl oz water
115-225 g/4-8 oz bacon, cut into small pieces (you can use gammon pieces)
1 tsp sugar
1½ tbsp plain flour
1½ tbsp oil
Dumplings:
1 egg
85 g/3 oz plain flour
65-85 g/2½-3 oz water
¼ tsp salt
1-2 tbsp fresh parsley, finely chopped (optional)

1 Drain the soaked beans, and place them in a large pan with fresh water. Add the bacon pieces and the sugar, and cook, simmering, for about 2 hours.
2 Make a brown roux: mix the flour with the oil, over low heat, stirring all the time until the paste turns brown and gives off a nutty aroma. Be careful not to let the flour burn. Have patience – this takes about 20-30 minutes.
3 Add a little of the soup liquid to the roux, and then pour the roux into the soup, stirring well. Let it cook a little longer on a low heat while you make the dumplings.
4 Make the dumplings: beat the egg, and, stirring, slowly add the other ingredients, including parsley, if liked. Beat to a stiff batter.
5 Bring the soup to the boil – you may need to add a little more water. Drop the dumplings by large spoonfuls into the boiling soup. Let them cook in the soup for about 15 minutes. Serve hot.

Right: Bean soup with dumplings

Beef barley soup

A thick 'farmhouse' soup, of the meal-in-a-bowl variety.

Serves: 4-6.
900 g/2 lb of stewing steak
3-4 sticks celery
3-4 tbsp fresh parsley, chopped
2 l/70 fl oz water
1 tbsp salt
2 tsp Worcester sauce
2 bay leaves
½ tsp thyme
2 small turnips, diced fairly small
115 g/4 oz barley

1 Cut the meat into smallish cubes. Chop the celery and parsley, and place in a pan with the meat and 1.7 l/60 fl oz of water, the salt, Worcester sauce, bay leaves and thyme. Simmer for 2 hours.
2 Chop the turnips. Remove the meat and celery pieces with a slotted spoon and set aside. Strain the stock, and return to the pan. Return the meat and celery, and add another 300 ml/10 fl oz water, the turnips and the barley. Simmer for another 30-45 minutes.
3 Adjust the seasoning and serve hot, with bread to mop up the gravy.

'Pigs in a blanket'

In some areas the name refers to oysters which are wrapped in a bacon 'blanket', then grilled and served on squares of hot buttered toast, but, in the Midwest at least, it means a rather tastier version of sausage rolls. Good for picnics or parties – children seem to love them.

Makes: 8 'pigs'.
8 frankfurters or other spicy or smoked sausages
tomato ketchup
mustard
Pastry:
225 g/8 oz plain white flour
1 tsp salt
1 tsp sugar
2½ tsp baking powder
50 g/2 oz butter or margarine
about 150 ml/5 fl oz milk
beaten egg for pastry glaze (optional)

1 Preheat the oven to 200°C/400°F/Gas Mark 6, and lightly grease a baking sheet.
2 Make the pastry: sift together the flour, salt, sugar, and baking powder. Cut in the fat and mix well. Add enough milk to give you a soft but not sticky dough.
3 Knead the dough a little before rolling out on a lightly floured surface. It should be about 5 mm/¼ in thick. Cut into rectangles the length of the sausages – 10 cm/4 in is about right – and wide enough to wrap around each.
4 Spread each pastry piece with tomato ketchup, and then with mustard. Lay the sausage on top, and roll, pinching the ends to seal. If you like, glaze the top with beaten egg. Place on the baking sheet, and cook for about 20 minutes, until golden brown.
Note: As they can be made with a variety of sausages, choose your favourite – they are good with spicy smoked German sausages and they need a tangy taste, so don't use good old British bangers.

Bratwurst in beer

What makes this dish a true Wisconsin-style recipe is the marinade – although it doesn't have a strong beer taste, you can tell when it's missing.

Serves: 4 as a main course.
8 bratwurst
600 ml/20 fl oz lager (or as much as is necessary to cover the wurst as a marinade)

1 Marinate the bratwurst in the lager for several hours.
2 Put the wurst and the lager into a saucepan and simmer gently for 20-30 minutes.
3 Heat the grill. Remove the wurst and place under the hot grill to brown. (Or barbecue it on hot coals and it is especially good!)
4 Serve hot with sauerkraut and fried potatoes, with lots of good German mustard, and some crusty dinner rolls; unless you are preparing this dish as part of a barbecue, when you just make it part of the spread.

Spare ribs and sauerkraut

Make some brown potatoes to go with this – it's a combination that really works. We've not made the sauerkraut. You can, of course, but it's a lengthy process. We draw the line here, and use the best canned or bottled variety we can find.

Serves: 4.
900 g/2 lb spare ribs
450-900 g/1-2 lb sauerkraut (depending on how much you like it)

1 Place the ribs in a pan with salted water to cover, and boil until almost tender.
2 Rinse the sauerkraut of brine, and drain. Place in a baking dish. Remove the ribs from their cooking liquid and place them on top of the sauerkraut (or, if you prefer, mix them). Add a little of the stock to moisten and give flavour – the dish shouldn't be too dry. Cook in the oven for about 1 hour at 180°C/350°F/Gas Mark 4.
3 Serve hot, with Brown potatoes (see page 98).

Tuna fish patties

These are very simple and, we think, rather tastier than you might imagine. If you burn them don't worry – the crispy burnt bits are even tastier!

Makes: about 7 patties.
2 × 185 g/6½ oz cans tuna, well drained
1 small onion, finely chopped
1-2 tsp fresh parsley, finely chopped
115 g/4 oz breadcrumbs
1 egg, beaten
½ tsp black pepper
vegetable oil for frying

1 Drain the tuna fish, and flake. Chop the onion and parsley, and mix with the tuna.
2 Add the breadcrumbs, egg, and seasoning. Mix well and mould into flattish patties about the size of hamburgers, and about 1 cm/½ in thick, or, if you prefer, shape into small balls, table-tennis size. These quantities give you about 21 balls.
3 In a large frying pan, pour a little oil and heat. Add the patties and fry gently, turning once, until browned all over. Add a little more oil if necessary, but try not to use too much – they aren't deep-fried.
4 Remove the patties and drain on absorbent paper.
5 Serve hot or cold.

Overleaf: Meatloaf (recipe, page 96): Cabbage & parsley salad (recipe, page 99)

Meatloaf

❛A real American family staple. Note that Midwestern cookery does not, as a rule, use a lot of seasoning. We give the recipes as they are cooked in the USA – adjust according to your taste. ❜

Serves: 4-6.
900 g/2 lb good quality minced beef
2 eggs
85 g/3 oz crushed water biscuits or matzos
85-115 g/3-4 oz dried breadcrumbs or oatflakes
225 ml/8 fl oz tomato juice
I small onion, finely chopped
I tsp salt
½ tsp black pepper

1 Mix all the ingredients in a bowl until well blended.
2 Put into a large loaf tin, patting the mixture down firmly so that the end-product will be a fairly close-textured loaf.
3 Bake for about 1-1½ hours, at 180°C/350°F/Gas Mark 4. The loaf should be brown on top.
4 To serve, turn out or leave in the pan, as you prefer. Slice, as you would bread. Serve hot, with mashed potatoes and seasonal vegetables, or cold with a slaw.

Sauerbrauten

❛This is a very good recipe for a party, or special dinner, but it does need advance planning – note the lengthy marinating time required! It's a deliciously different way of cooking your joint, and actually very simple to do. The meat has a very slightly sour taste without being vinegary, and the gravy is thick, creamy without being cloying, and piquant. You can use any size of beef joint so long as you have pans large enough to cope. ❜

Serves: 4.
900 g/2 lb roasting joint of beef
vegetable oil for browning meat
2 medium to large tomatoes, sliced or I small can tomatoes
3 tbsp flour or cornflour, mixed to a paste with 2-3 tbsp cold water
4 ginger biscuits, broken (or crushed)
150 ml/5 fl oz sour cream
Marinade:
225 ml/8 fl oz cider vinegar
225 ml/8 fl oz water
I small onion, cut into wedges
I carrot
2 sprigs celery leaves
1½ tsp salt
4-6 cloves, whole
I large bay leaf
4-6 black peppercorns
4-6 juniper berries

1 Mix the marinade: cut the onion into wedges and separate the pieces. Very thinly slice the carrot. Mix all the ingredients in a pan and bring to the boil. Cover and simmer for 15 minutes, and leave to cool.
2 Place the beef in a bowl, pour in the marinade to cover the meat. If you need more liquid, add water. Cover and leave for at least 3 days (5 days if you keep it in the refrigerator) – Kenna usually marinates the meat for I week.
3 Remove the meat from the marinade and dry it off gently.
4 Heat the oil in a cast-iron casserole dish or heavy-bottomed pan, and brown the meat.
5 Slice the tomatoes, and place around the meat. (If using canned, break them up a bit – you can use the juice too.) Add the vegetables from the marinade, and about 300 ml/10 fl oz of the liquid, reserving the remainder (you may need to add more later). Cover the pan and simmer gently for about I hour.
6 Remove the meat from the pan, and keep warm. Mix the flour and water paste, and add to the gravy, stirring until the sauce thickens.
7 Break the ginger biscuits into smallish pieces, and add to the sauce, mashing them in when they go soggy. (If you prefer, you can crush them first.)
8 Gently stir in the sour cream.
9 To serve, slice the meat thinly, and top with the sauce, accompanied by plain boiled potatoes. If you have any sauce left over try slicing potatoes thinly, and baking them in the sauce – they taste very good!

Midwestern chop suey

A 'Chinese' dish, apparently unknown in China! It is said to have been created by the Chinese labourers working on the railway line across America, and this is the Midwestern version.

Serves: 4.
450 g/I lb meat, either boneless lean pork or stewing beef – best if you use 225 g/8 oz each
2 tbsp oil
4 sticks celery, coarsely chopped into 2.5-4 cm/I-I½ in pieces
2 onions, chopped
350 g/I2 oz fresh beansprouts (or equivalent canned – fresh are crunchier)
2 tsp sugar
2 tbsp soy sauce
120 ml/4 fl oz water
I tsp salt
I tsp black pepper
I tbsp cornflour, mixed to a paste with 1-2 tbsp water
noodles (flat variety are best) or rice, if you prefer

1 Cut the meat into thin I cm/½ in pieces, and put in a pan to brown in the oil.
2 Chop the celery, and onions, and when the meat is browned, reduce the heat to low, add the vegetables and cook for about 10 minutes.
3 Add the beansprouts, sugar, soy sauce, and water. Cover and cook for about another 10 minutes.
4 Add the seasoning, and mix the cornflour to a paste. Stir in. It will quickly thicken the sauce. Leave on a gentle heat while the noodles are cooked.
5 Boil the noodles in lightly salted water until they are *al dente*. Drain well, and serve topped with the meat sauce.

Hungarian goulash

Every Slavic group has its own recipe for goulash – here is the Hungarian version, US style. It's debatable whether they would recognize it in Budapest!

Serves: 4.
450 g/I lb stewing beef
I medium onion
2 cloves garlic
2 tbsp oil
I½ tbsp paprika
I tsp salt
200 g/7 oz can tomatoes
2-4 potatoes

1 Cut the beef into 2.5 cm/I in cubes. Chop the onions and garlic, and brown with the beef in oil, in a heavy-bottomed pan or cast-iron casserole.
2 Add the paprika, salt, and the tomatoes, breaking them up a bit – pour in their juice too – and add water until the liquid covers the meat. Simmer for about I hour.
3 Cut the potatoes (peeled, or not, as you choose) into chunks. Add to the goulash and cook for a further ½ hour or so, until the potatoes are cooked.
4 Serve hot. The traditional side dish is cabbage, and you need some good fresh bread to mop up the gravy.

Brown potatoes

❝Or, Every Small Boy's Dream! ❞

Serves: 6-8.
6 medium potatoes
4 cloves garlic, crushed
1-2 tsp salt
1 tsp black pepper
about 675 g/1½ lb baked beans (1 × 425 g/15 oz can plus 1 × 200 g/7 oz can)

1 Peel the potatoes, chop and boil. When soft, drain and place in a mixing bowl.
2 Add the crushed garlic, seasoning, and the baked beans. Mash all together well, and serve hot.

Cabbage and noodles

❝This is a pretty basic recipe which responds well to being dressed up. If you are particularly fond of cabbage it makes a warming lunch dish – put in crispy crumbled bacon pieces, or stir in some yoghurt or sour cream, and add some herbs during cooking. ❞

Serves: 4-6 as a side dish, making generous servings.
1 medium (or ½ large) head green cabbage
1 large onion
4 tbsp fat (preferably pork or chicken)
salt and pepper to taste
225 g/8 oz egg noodles – flat noodles are best

1 Chop the cabbage and onion fairly coarsely, and put into a saucepan. Add the fat, and season. Cover and cook until the cabbage is soft, stirring occasionally.
2 Add the noodles to boiling lightly salted water, and cook until *al dente*. Drain well.
3 Add the noodles to the cabbage and mix well. Serve with lots of freshly ground black pepper.

German potato salad

❝This is a salad with a rather unusual taste, a good side dish much served at barbecues, 'pot-lucks', parties, or any family meal. As to its name – it must have come over with the German immigrants, but Kenna, who has also lived in Germany, says she's never had it there! ❞

Serves: 6-8.
6 medium-large potatoes
6 slices streaky bacon, cut into smallish pieces
1 large onion, finely diced
175 ml/6 fl oz water
50-85 ml/2-3 fl oz cider vinegar
2 tbsp flour
1½ tbsp granulated sugar
1½ tsp salt
1 tsp black pepper

1 Boil the potatoes whole.
2 While the potatoes are cooking, fry the bacon until crisp, and drain on absorbent paper. Re-serve the bacon fat.
3 Finely dice the onion and fry in the bacon fat.
4 Mix the water with the vinegar and have ready to hand.
5 When the onions are tender, add the flour and stir in well. Add the sugar, salt and pepper, and then the water-vinegar mix. Stir until you have a smooth paste, cooking over a low heat.
6 When the potatoes are cooked, drain, and pull off the skins. Slice the potatoes and place in a serving dish. Crumble the bacon over the potatoes, and pour on the warm dressing. Mix gently and serve immediately.

Cabbage and parsley salad

A coleslaw variation – sweetish, sharpish, simple.

Serves: 4.
½ head of cabbage, green or white
2 bunches fresh parsley
I large onion, finely sliced
Dressing:
3 tbsp white sugar
I-2 tsp salt
2 tsp black pepper
6 tbsp cider vinegar
4 tbsp light vegetable or salad oil

1 Shred the cabbage, roughly chop the parsley, and mix together.
2 Finely chop the onion and add to the slaw.
3 Make the dressing: mix all the ingredients, pour onto the salad, and toss. Chill before serving.

Hot lettuce salad

A simple but nicely different way of making a lettuce salad. We do advise that you use the iceberg lettuce: the heart of a cos might do, but don't make this with round lettuce.

Serves: 4 as a side dish, or 2 as a light lunch, served with bread.
I small-medium head iceberg lettuce
4 slices streaky bacon, cut into small pieces
50 ml/2 fl oz water
50 ml/2 fl oz cider vinegar
I tsp sugar
½ tsp salt

1 Cut the bacon and fry gently until crisp. Reserve the fat, and drain the bacon on absorbent paper.
2 Coarsely chop the lettuce and put into a serving bowl.
3 In a separate bowl, mix the water and the vinegar, stirring in the sugar and salt. Add it to the bacon fat and bring to the boil. Pour over the lettuce and toss so it is well covered.
Serving suggestion: For a more substantial dish, place a slice of toasted garlic bread in each individual serving bowl and top with a portion of the salad, pouring in enough dressing to soak into the toast a little.

Kidney bean salad with boiled dressing

This was Friday's meal – Grandma served this salad, beans piled high on a lettuce-lined platter, garnished with slices of hard-boiled egg around the edge. It is very substantial and really needs nothing more than some good homemade bread.

Serves: 4-6.
225-275 g/8-10 oz dried red kidney beans, soaked overnight or 2 X 425 g/15 oz cans red
kidney beans
I small onion, finely chopped
2 sticks celery, finely chopped
3 large dill cucumbers, finely chopped
Dressing:
I egg
120 ml/4 fl oz cider vinegar
115 g/4 oz granulated or caster sugar

1 If using dried beans, soak them overnight. Red kidney beans contain a toxic substance. To remove this, it is essential to boil the beans vigorously for the first 10 minutes. Then boil until soft. Drain and cool.
2 Chop the onion, celery and dill cucumbers, and mix with the beans.
3 Make the dressing: beat the egg with the vinegar and sugar. Heat in a saucepan, bring to the boil, and stir until it thickens. Allow to cool before pouring over the bean salad. Chill.
Note: The dressing is rather sweet. We have reduced the sugar (in line with British tastes) – add or reduce still further as you wish.

German chocolate cake with coconut pecan frosting

‘Well, no, you won't find this one in Germany! In the States, there is a sweetened light chocolate known as German baking chocolate, which is used for this cake, but cocoa works well as a substitute. What makes the cake a bit special is the icing. Traditionally this cake is iced between the layers and on top, but not around the sides. ’

4 heaped tbsp cocoa
120 ml/4 fl oz boiling water
225 ml/8 fl oz buttermilk
1 tsp bicarbonate of soda
400 g/14 oz granulated sugar
225 g/8 oz margarine, softened
4 large eggs, separated
275 g/10 oz plain white flour
1 tsp salt
2 tsp vanilla essence
Frosting:
175 ml/6 fl oz milk
225 g/8 oz granulated sugar
3 egg yolks
115 g/4 oz margarine
1 tsp vanilla essence
150 g/5 oz coconut, desiccated or shredded
50-85 g/2-3 oz pecan nuts (or walnuts), chopped

1 Preheat the oven to 180°C/350°F/Gas Mark 4. Grease and flour 2 × 23 cm/9 in sandwich tins.
2 Mix the cocoa with the boiling water and set aside.
3 Place the buttermilk in a fairly large bowl and add the bicarbonate of soda (it will froth up). Now set it aside.
4 Cream together the sugar and the margarine. Add the egg yolks. Now add the flour and the salt, alternately with the buttermilk.
5 Add the vanilla essence, and the cocoa liquid, and beat well.
6 Whisk the egg whites until stiff and fold into the cake mixture. Pour into the cake tins and bake for 40-50 minutes. Cool before icing.
7 Make the frosting: in a saucepan, mix the milk, sugar, egg yolks, margarine and vanilla. Bring to the boil, reduce heat a little and cook for 10-12 minutes, stirring constantly. Remove from the heat and mix in the coconut and chopped nuts. Spread on the cooled cake and leave to set.

Rhubarb torte

'An unusual version of a rhubarb pie – the fruit doesn't really set but oozes luscious goo into a crumble-like base. The nuts make the real difference! '

Serves: 8-10.
Pastry base:
225 g/8 oz plain white flour
1 tsp baking powder
2 tbsp white sugar
½ tsp salt
115 g/4 oz butter or margarine
50-85 g/2-3 oz walnuts, finely chopped
2 egg yolks, lightly beaten
Filling:
about 900 g/1 lb rhubarb sticks (be generous), cut into 1 cm/½ in lengths
2 egg yolks
225 g/8 oz granulated sugar
40-50 g/1½-2 oz flour
Meringue topping:
4 egg whites
½ tsp salt
pinch of cream of tartar
1 tsp vanilla essence
115 g/4 oz caster sugar

1 Make the pastry base: mix the flour, baking powder, sugar and salt. Work in the fat, using a pastry blender or your fingers. Preheat the oven to 180°C/350°F/Gas Mark 4.

2 Chop the walnuts and add to the pastry mixture along with the egg yolks. Mix well, and pat into the baking dish or tin. (This is a rather dry mixture – don't worry.)

3 Cut the rhubarb. Mix the egg yolks, flour and sugar, and add to the rhubarb. Fill the pastry crust, and bake, uncovered for 20 minutes. Cover and cook for a further 15-20 minutes, or until the rhubarb is cooked.

4 While the pie is baking, make the meringue topping: beat the egg whites with salt, vanilla essence and cream of tartar until you have stiffish peaks. Beat in the sugar until you have a thick and glossy mixture. Remove the pie from the oven, and pile the meringue on top, smoothing and shaping as you wish. Return to the oven and bake at 170°C/325°F/Gas Mark 3 for 20 minutes or so. The top should be just turning golden.

Overleaf: German chocolate cake with coconut pecan frosting and Scripture cake (recipe, page 104)

Applesauce cake

‘A lightly spiced, dense and moist cake. ’

Makes: 2 loaves. Or, use a deep 25 cm/10 in square tin.
3 large cooking apples (Bramleys)
a little sugar
225 g/8 oz butter or margarine
350 g/12 oz brown sugar (preferably dark, but you can use light brown)
2 eggs, beaten
400 g/14 oz plain white flour
2 tsp bicarbonate of soda
1 tsp salt
2 tsp ground cinnamon
1 tsp ground cloves
350 g/12 oz raisins
175-225 g/6-8 oz walnuts, chopped

1 Preheat the oven to 180°C/350°F/Gas Mark 4. Lightly grease and flour two loaf tins or one deep 25 cm/10 in square tin.
2 Peel, core, and slice the apples. Stew gently, in water, with a little sugar, until soft. (Don't use too much water, and drain carefully, or you'll have a rather sloppy mixture.)
3 Meanwhile, in a large bowl, cream the butter/margarine and sugar, and stir in the eggs.
4 Add the dry ingredients and mix well.
5 Add the raisins. (If you like, plump them first by putting them in a colander over a pan of steaming water. Leave for a few minutes, and pat off the excess moisture with a kitchen towel – it helps to stop them sinking.)
6 Chop the walnuts and add to the mixture.
7 When the apples are ready, drain, and mash to a pulp. Stir into the cake mixture, beating well. Turn out into the tins.
8 Bake at 180°C/350°F/Gas Mark 4 for 1½ hours. Leave to cool before turning out.
Serving suggestion: This cake is sometimes iced with Cream cheese frosting (see our recipe on page 143). We don't bother, preferring it plain – it's quite rich enough!

Scripture cake

‘No doubt that this one comes from the Bible Belt. It's a fairly light fruit cake, gently spicy, and the figs make a pleasant change. ’

175 g/6 oz butter (Psalms 55:21)
225 g/8 oz sugar (sweet cane from a far country – Jeremiah 6:20)
3 eggs (Isaiah 10:14)
225 g/8 oz plain flour (I Kings 4:22)
pinch of salt (Luke 14:34)
1 tsp baking powder (a little leaven – I Corinthians 5:6)
¼ tsp nutmeg (spices – II Chronicles 9:9)
1 tsp allspice
1 tsp ground cloves
2 tsp ground cinnamon
50 ml/2 fl oz milk (Judges 4:19)
1 tbsp honey (Judges 14:18)
175 g/6 oz raisins (II Samuel 16:1)
150 g/5 oz figs, chopped (Song of Solomon 2:13)
85 g/3 oz almonds, blanched and slivered (Numbers 17:8)

1 Preheat the oven to 170°C/325°F/Gas Mark 3. Grease a loaf tin.
2 Cream the butter and the sugar until fluffy. Beat the eggs and mix in well.
3 Sift the flour with the salt, baking powder, and all the spices, and add alternately with the milk. Stir in the honey – if it isn't too runny, warm it gently first.
4 Stir in the raisins, chopped figs, and the nuts, and mix well.
5 Pour into the loaf tin and bake for about 1½ hours (or until done when tested). Let it cool in the tin for about 30 minutes before turning out on to a rack to cool thoroughly. This cake keeps well wrapped in foil, or stored in an airtight tin. It freezes well too.

Potica

Pronounced 'poteetsa', this is a delicious, rather cake-like tea-bread, with a wonderfully nutty paste filling. It makes a regular appearance on the festival table be it Christmas or Easter, a wedding, a family reunion, or any special gathering.

Makes: 2 large rolls (Swiss-roll shaped).
Dough:
275 g/10 oz butter or margarine plus a few knobs for the top
175 ml/6 fl oz milk
2 tbsp dried yeast
120 ml/4 fl oz warm water
675 g/1½ lb plain white flour plus flour for rolling out
½ tsp salt
3 tbsp sugar
4 egg yolks
Filling:
450 g/1 lb walnuts, minced or ground
175 g/6 oz raisins/sultanas
4 tbsp white sugar
1 tsp ground cinnamon
150 ml/5 fl oz milk
4 egg whites
225 g/8 oz sugar, caster or granulated

1 Melt the butter/margarine, mix with the milk, and allow to cool.
2 Mix the yeast in warm water and set aside.
3 Mix the flour, salt and sugar in a large bowl.
4 Stir the beaten egg yolks into the melted butter mixture and add into the flour. Add the yeast mixture, and beat all together well until you have a soft sticky dough which holds its shape.
5 Leave the dough in the bowl, cover and place in the refrigerator for a few hours, or overnight.
6 Make the filling: grind the nuts to a paste and place in a saucepan. Add the raisins, sugar, cinnamon, and milk. Over gentle heat, blend to a smooth paste.
7 Beat the egg whites until they are fairly stiff and then beat in the sugar. Fold in the paste and mix through gently.
8 Roll in dough: on a table or large work surface spread an old, clean sheet or other cloth, and dust with flour. Place the dough in the centre, and roll out into a rectangle. Use a rolling pin, and go gently, working outwards until it's about 38 cm/15 in wide, 50-60 cm/20-24 in long and about 3 mm/¼ in thick.
9 Spread the nut paste over the dough, leaving a 5 cm/2 in border around three sides, spreading up to the edge on one long side. Roll up from this side into a long fat sausage, and pinch the ends together to seal.
10 Slice the roll in half, and place the two sausages in a 23×30 cm/ 9×12 in baking tin. Cover and set to rise in a warm place for 1 hour.
11 Preheat the oven to 180°C/350°F/Gas Mark 4. Dot the top of the potica with little knobs of butter and bake for ¾-1 hour, or until golden-brown and firm to the touch.
12 Allow to cool (if you can restrain yourself – we find it almost impossible). It *is* better cold. Turn out, and serve with butter, or just as it comes. To store, wrap in foil and keep in the fridge.

Grandma's Slovenian strudel

'This is a chunkier and less sweet version of the better known Austrian apfel strudel. It makes a lot, but in our experience it tends to disappear rather quickly! (It also freezes well.) Don't be put off by the seemingly endless instructions – just take it step by step and you'll find it's really quite simple. '

Makes: 20 good-sized portions.
Dough:
350 g/12 oz plain white flour plus flour for rolling
½ tsp salt
50 g/2 oz butter or margarine, melted
50 ml/2 fl oz light vegetable oil
1 egg, beaten
175 ml/6 fl oz warm water
Filling:
8 medium apples
350 g/12 oz cottage cheese
2 eggs
115 g/4 oz granulated sugar plus about 115 g/4 oz for sprinkling
1 tsp vanilla essence
50 g/2 oz butter or margarine, melted
115 g/4 oz day-old breadcrumbs or crushed digestive biscuits
about 175 g/6 oz raisins or sultanas
about 2 tbsp ground cinnamon
butter knobs for top of strudel
icing sugar to dredge

1 Put the flour, with salt, into a mixing bowl, and make a well in the centre.
2 Melt the butter/margarine and mix with the vegetable oil. Add the warm water and the beaten egg, mix together and pour into the well. Mix to form a very soft dough. Knead gently until it is smooth and silky soft, not sticky. Leave in the bowl, cover, and place in the refrigerator for 1 hour.
3 Peel, core, and thinly slice the apples. Set aside.
4 In a bowl, mix the cottage cheese, eggs, 115 g/4 oz sugar, and vanilla. Set aside.
5 Melt the butter/margarine, and mix into the breadcrumbs/crushed biscuits. Set aside.
6 Roll the dough: you need space – a work surface covered with an old clean sheet, spread with a dusting of flour. Have the baking tin or tray ready. Preheat the oven to 170°C/325°F/Gas Mark 3.
7 Place the dough in the centre of the rolling surface. Stretch into a rectangle and, using a rolling pin at this stage, gently work on the dough increasing the size and decreasing the thickness. It is very pliable. Be careful not to tear it, though don't worry overmuch about the odd little hole. Turn the dough over, and continue rolling and gently stretching.
8 When it's about 40 cm/18 in wide by 90 cm /36 in long, abandon the rolling pin, and use your hands. Stretch as thinly as possible without tearing (if you do, patch it later – it's not ideal but no one will notice). Lift one side of the dough to get one hand underneath it, and, starting from the middle, very gently stroke the underside with your fingers. Slowly work your way all around it. When the dough is about 60 cm/24 in by 120 cm/48 in and opaque, you've done it! Don't worry if you can't get it to such a large size the first time – it takes some practice. Just make it smaller, patch the tears, and carry on – it will taste just fine.
9 Spread the apple slices more or less evenly over the pastry – you don't have to cover every inch! The simplest way is to just cover the area, but if you want to bother, and if you know the lengths you will have to cut the strudel into to fit your tin, it is possible to cut the pastry at this stage, so that you make up 2-3 smaller strudel rather than one large one. If you are doing this, cover the area of the dough in 2-3 'blocks', leaving 'borders'.
10 Sprinkle the breadcrumbs/biscuits over the dough.
11 Sprinkle the sugar all over the apples and then follow with a liberal shower of cinnamon – it takes quite a lot.
12 Next spread the raisins, and finally the cottage cheese mixture – don't even attempt to spread it evenly, just sprinkle dollops.
13 Roll the strudel: Carefully pick up one side of the sheet, and lift it gently. Allow the edge of the dough nearest to you to flick itself over into the beginning of a roll. As you raise the sheet, the rest will follow, slowly turning itself into a loosely packed 'sausage'. If you prefer, fold the side edges in before you start to roll to create neatly parcelled ends. If you don't bother with this, just pinch the ends to seal, and, if you have holes, pull a bit off the end pastry and use to patch.
14 With a sharp knife slice the strudel into lengths to fit your pan, and reseal each end by pinching the dough.
15 Dot the top with butter knobs, and bake at 170°C/325°F/Gas Mark 3 for 1 hour.
16 Serve warm or cold sprinkled with icing sugar. It's best after a couple of days – wrap in foil and store in the refrigerator.

Right: Grandma's Slovenian strudel

chapter

6.

The North-East

New England
& the
Mid-Atlantic States

*M*ost people know of the Pilgrim Fathers and the 'Mayflower': they settled in this area – hence New England – and founded the original thirteen colonies where began what is now the United States of America. We've grown a lot since then, and have undergone many changes. You've heard tell of the Boston Tea Party, the War of Independence, and 4 July 1776 – independent we became, but the cultural influences and traditions remain.

Of course, the English weren't the only settlers – the Dutch came too. New York's island, Manhattan, was once called New Amsterdam, and later other groups arrived, often, as with those early pilgrims, seeking religious freedom. One such group is the Amish. Their communities are now found in Ohio and Indiana too, but more commonly take their name from the state where they have perhaps the greatest concentration: they are also called the Pennsylvania Dutch. This is in fact a corruption of 'Deutsch', for they were German in origin, though their leader was actually Swiss – one Jacob Amman (hence 'Amish'), a man of rigid and conservative views. The Amish, or 'plain folks', have continued most diligently in the life they have always known; farming. They grow and raise most of their own food on some of America's richest farmland. They have a severe style of dress, eschewing zip fasteners in favour of buttons and ties; and they drive horse-drawn carriages rather than cars or other motor vehicles. We have included a few Amish 'plain' recipes.

Everyone has an image of New York City – 'the Big Apple' – it's practically part of British cultural heritage too: Harlem, Manhattan, the Bronx, Coney Island, Fifth Avenue and Broadway, Central Park and Times Square, skyscrapers and hustle-bustle. I remember my naivety as a youngster in thinking that New York City and New York State were one and the same (and I was not alone). Then I started university and made a friend from 'upstate' New York. To the surprise of us all, she was terrified of subways and the cars and crowds of the city! Rather more recently, I drove through the state up to Vermont for a skiing holiday: beyond the city lie miles and miles of lush green countryside and, even further north, the tranquillity of the Maine coast. Here, the seasons are distinct: people come from far and wide to see the New England falls (autumns), particularly spectacular in Vermont and New Hampshire, and I know of no one who has been disappointed!

Traditional New England cooking is very close to traditional English (and probably Irish) cooking. Where they seem too alike, we've not included the recipes, but many have undergone gentle adaptation. Much of the New England economy was based on its fishing – seafood is still plentiful and cheap, and extremely popular. I've yet to eat a lobster tastier than those of Maine. These, the clams, and other *seafood are transported all over the USA. Of course clambakes are well-known events: huge quantities of the shellfish are baked in their shells on a circle of flat stones which have been heated by a log fire. The logs are raked off, the stones covered with fresh seaweed on which the clams and anything else to be baked – jacket potatoes, corn on the cob – are laid. Another layer of seaweed is added and the whole covered with sailcloth pegged down with more stones, to keep in the heat. Two to three hours later, it's ready to eat! Nowadays it is probably more common to cook the clams in large steamers, but the seaweed is still employed as a filter and moistener. We could have filled the book with these superb local recipes but since seafood is hardly cheap here, we've restricted ourselves to including just enough to give you the taste.*

New York and Washington D.C., in particular, are international cities with many different ethnic communities adding to the richness of 'north-eastern' food. These ethnic recipes, by and large, we've not represented: they are better served elsewhere. We've tried, rather, to capture the spirit of traditional New England cooking, so this is the section to choose from when you are entertaining guests who like to stay within the realms of the known (more or less) when it comes to eating. It's the safest – not too spicy, not too sweet, not too salty (except for the corned beef boiled dinner), neither heavy nor too light – just honest-to-goodness fare, and closest to home!

Hot crab dip

'Quick to make, and impressive to serve, this is rich, creamy, and fairly delicate in taste – true New England style. '

Serves: 4.
225 g/8 oz crab meat (best fresh rather than canned) or 10-12 crab sticks
225 g/8 oz cream cheese
2 tbsp mayonnaise
I egg
I tbsp vermouth, or dry sherry, or white wine
2 tbsp onion, finely chopped (optional)
2 tbsp green pepper, finely chopped (optional)

1 Heat the oven to 180°C/250°F/Gas Mark 4.
2 Mix together the cream cheese and mayonnaise.
3 Beat an egg with the vermouth and add to the cheese mixture.
4 Flake the crab meat/sticks, and mix with the cheese.
5 Finely chop the onion and green pepper, mix in, and pour into a small ovenproof dish. Bake for 15 minutes.
6 Serve hot, with wheat crackers.
Serving suggestion: Don't be tempted to serve it cold – it's really so much better hot. If you prefer, this could be spooned on to a bed of lettuce and served with a wedge of lemon. It would also make a delicious filling for vol-au-vents, served warm and crumbly.

New England clam chowder

'This is a fairly thick and creamy soup with a rather delicate taste. On the Eastern seaboard clams are plentiful and would be used fresh, but here we've used canned clams. Chowders may be made with other types of seafood or any white fish, or a mixture of both. '

Serves: 4 as a starter.
4 slices streaky bacon
2 onions, chopped
I × 385 g/13 oz can clams
2 tbsp flour
450-600 ml/15-20 fl oz milk
4 medium potatoes
2 bay leaves
black pepper

1 Fry the bacon gently, and remove the pieces. Drain on absorbent paper.
2 Chop the onion and sauté in bacon fat (adding more fat if necessary).
3 Drain the clams, reserving the liquid, which is made up to 450 ml/15 fl oz with milk. Chop the clams if necessary. Add the clams to the onions and sauté for a few minutes.
4 Add the flour and gradually stir in the liquid.
5 Chop the potatoes and add to the pot, with bay leaves and pepper to taste. Cut the bacon into small pieces and add to the soup. Cover and simmer until the potatoes are cooked. If necessary, add more liquid – up to another 150 ml/5 fl oz of milk.
6 Serve hot.

Right: New England clam chowder

Thick onion soup

'Thick it certainly is, rich and creamy. If you like onions, you'll love it, and it's quite easy to make. '

Serves: 4-6.
6 medium onions
65 g/2½ oz butter or margarine
750 ml/25 fl oz water
3 tbsp flour
450 ml/15 fl oz milk
salt
½-1 tsp cayenne
1 egg yolk
grated cheese for topping

1 Chop the onions and sauté them in about 25 g/1 oz butter/margarine, for 5 minutes or so. Add the water, and let it simmer for about 30 minutes. Remove from the heat and allow it to cool slightly. You now have a choice: if you like a smooth soup, purée the onions in a blender, or push them through a sieve. If you prefer the 'bits', leave it as it is.
2 Make a roux with about 40 g/1½ oz butter/margarine and 3 tablespoons flour. Stir in the milk, add the seasonings, and stir until the sauce thickens. Add to the onion mixture.
3 Lightly beat the egg yolk and stir into the soup. Mix thoroughly. It may be necessary to reheat gently but make sure that the soup does not boil.
4 Serve hot, with a little grated cheese sprinkled on top.

Amish mock kidney soup

'We would like to be able to explain just why this is called 'mock kidney' rather than simply 'liver soup', but unfortunately, we don't know. It is a most surprisingly delicate light broth with a delicious flavour. '

Serves: 4-6.
225 g/8 oz calves' liver (or lambs')
1 slice streaky bacon
1 onion
50 g/2 oz butter
1 large carrot
1 turnip
1 stick celery
2 handfuls fresh parsley, coarsely chopped
1 tsp thyme
1 tsp marjoram
salt and pepper to taste
2 l/70 fl oz water
2 tbsp flour or cornflour
1 tbsp tomato ketchup

1 Chop the liver, bacon, and onion into small pieces, and sauté in butter for 5 minutes or so. Use a heavy-bottomed saucepan large enough to hold all the ingredients.
2 Chop the carrot, turnip, celery, and parsley, and add, with the other herbs and seasonings. Add the water, bring to the boil, skim off the fat, and simmer for 1 hour.
3 Strain the soup, reserving the liquid, which is returned to the pan. Pick out the pieces of liver and jettison the rest.
4 Purée the liver. Use a mouli or blender – if the latter, add a little of the broth.
5 Mix the flour/cornflour with about 2 tablespoons of the broth (now a little cooled), and stir the paste into the broth with the liver purée. Add the tomato ketchup and heat through, stirring. The broth will thicken only slightly.
6 Serve hot, with some good bread to help soak up this most delicious soup.

Codfish balls

Makes: about 16 balls.
350 g/12 oz cod
about 350 g/12 oz potatoes (2 medium potatoes)
1 small onion, grated
salt and pepper to taste
1 egg
flour for coating
oil for frying

'Also known as Cape Cod turkey, this is a popular Boston brunch and it is usual to make it with salt cod. This is available here from stores which cater for the Afro-Caribbean trade in particular, but we have adapted the recipe to fresh cod. The fish balls are surprisingly light and delicate, and should be served with lemon mayonnaise (see recipe below) which adds a deliciously creamy sharpness and tang. '

1 Poach or boil the cod until tender. Drain, remove skin and bones, and flake the fish.
2 Peel and boil the potatoes. When soft, drain well, and mash.
3 Mix the cod with the mash. Grate the onion, and add, along with the seasoning.
4 Bind the mixture with raw egg. You need a fairly thick consistency for rolling into balls, but don't have it too dry. You may need to add another egg, or a little milk. Take tablespoons of the mixture, mould into balls and roll in flour until they are well coated.
5 Heat oil in a frying pan to about 5 mm/¼ in depth. Fry the balls, a few at a time, turning every now and then, to brown all over. Remove and drain on absorbent paper. Keep warm until you have fried all the balls.
6 Serve hot, or warm, with lemon mayonnaise (which tastes best slightly chilled), and garnish with lemon wedges. If you want to make the fish balls look very pretty, pile into a pyramid and decorate with sprigs of parsley, or what you will.

Lemon mayonnaise

Makes: about 450 ml/15 fl oz.
2 egg yolks
about 1-1½ tsp salt
about 1-2 tsp black pepper
½ tsp mustard
juice of 1 lemon
300 ml/10 fl oz oil
finely grated rind of ½ lemon

'This may be made with olive oil, but I find the taste too strong and prefer to use some other, like sunflower. '

1 Beat the yolks with a little salt and pepper. Don't put in all the seasoning at this stage – reserve to adjust later.
2 Beat in the mustard and about 1 teaspoon lemon juice.
3 Drop by drop, add about 50-85 ml/2-3 fl oz oil, beating all the time.
4 Add another 1-2 teaspoons lemon juice, and beat in, adding more oil. From this stage you can beat in more oil at a time. Beat until all is well incorporated.
5 Adjust the seasoning – add the rest of the lemon juice if you like (we do). Beat in the lemon rind. Chill before serving – you will find that the lemon flavour develops, and by the time you serve the mayonnaise, it will have a most delicious zing.

Amish oatmeal pancakes

'These pancakes are rather more the 'drop' kind, but if you want them thinner (and larger) add more milk. They are good with coffee or tea, the oaty taste makes a nice change. '

Makes: about 12.
450 ml/15 fl oz milk
115 g/4 oz oatflakes
1 tbsp flour
2½ tsp baking powder
1 tsp salt
1 tbsp butter, melted
1-2 eggs, separated
1 tbsp sugar

1 Use a griddle or heavy-bottomed frying pan. Heat it well, and lightly oil the surface.
2 Heat the milk, add the oatflakes, stir and leave to cool. We use porridge oats. It is apparently less common in the USA to differentiate between flakes and meal – use whichever, and use your judgement about the consistency.
3 Mix the flour, baking powder and salt in with the oatflakes.
4 Set the fat to melt. Stir in the beaten egg yolks, then add the melted fat. Add the sugar.
5 Beat the egg whites until they are stiff. Fold into the oatflake mixture.
6 Drop tablespoons of the batter on to the hot griddle. They will spread a little. When the surface begins to bubble slightly, turn and brown the other side.
7 Serve hot, with syrup, brown sugar, fruit purée, or just lots of butter, and, if you like, a good fruity jam.

Potato knishes

'A sort of cross between a pasty and a dumpling, the knish comes originally from Russia and Eastern Europe, and is a well-loved Jewish snack. In New York City it is sold from street stalls in rather the same way that hot dogs are in London. We like ours well-filled, but you can get away with lesser amounts for the filling than we have given here. You can of course vary the fillings – try chopped chicken pieces, or beef, or lots of grated cheese with onion. You might even like to try a sweet version, with fruit or filled with jam. '

Makes: about 12.
4 medium potatoes
2 eggs
1 tsp salt
1 tsp black pepper
6 tbsp flour plus flour for rolling dough
oil for frying
Filling:
225 g/8 oz chicken livers
1-2 medium onions
1 tbsp fat

1 Put the potatoes on to boil, whole. When done, drain, and cool a little before removing the skins. Mash the potatoes well, and set aside.
2 Prepare the filling: chop the onions and sauté in the fat. When they are beginning to brown add the chicken livers, stir round and cook them through. They don't take long. Break them up a bit by stirring. When they have cooked, remove from the heat and set aside.
3 Beat the eggs and mix with the mash. Add the seasoning. Gradually add flour to thicken until you have a fairly soft dough.
4 Flour a surface and roll out the dough to about 5 mm/¼ in thick. Cut into squares of about 12.5-15 cm/5-6 in. Place some filling in the centre, fold over, and crimp the edges to seal. (Excess dough can be cut off and rolled out again.)
5 Heat the oil in a frying pan – about 1 cm/½ in depth will do (or you can use more and truly deep fry). Place the knishes gently in the hot fat. As they brown, turn them. Remove and drain on absorbent paper.
6 Serve hot. They are wonderful with a dollop of sour cream or yoghurt!
Note: You can make the knishes much smaller if you prefer – they are then rather good to serve as snacks with drinks. Although we've not done them this way, we're told they can be baked in the oven (low heat) for about 30 minutes if you don't like to fry them.

Right: Amish oatmeal pancakes

New England codfish hash

'Lighter than it may seem on reading the recipe, and very simple, this makes a lovely lunch dish, excellent with Harvard beets. It would also be good with fried eggs for a hearty breakfast. '

Serves: 4.
450 g/I lb cod
4 medium potatoes
I small onion, finely chopped
I-2 tsp salt
I-2 tsp black pepper
I-2 tsp cayenne
II5 g/4 oz streaky bacon

1 Boil the potatoes. Drain, and remove the skins. Coarsely chop the potatoes.
2 Gently poach or boil the fish until tender. Drain, remove the skin and bones, and flake the fish, but don't break it up too much.
3 Chop the onion and mix with the fish and potatoes, and add the seasoning.
4 Fry the bacon until you have extracted as much fat as possible. Discard the bacon.
5 Let the fat get very hot. (You may need to add more fat.) Add the fish mixture, stirring it lightly in the pan. Gently pat it down and fry without stirring until the underside is well browned.
6 Serve hot.

Lobster American-style

'Not to be confused with Homard a l'Americaine, or l'Amoricaine, with the rival claims for invention and the controversy over its origins and spelling. This way of serving lobster is so very simple one hardly needs a recipe and lobster is such a very delicious meat that to dress it up any more seems to us a crime. '

Use: about 225-350 g/8-12 oz lobster per person.
boiled lobster – allow 225-350 g/8-12 oz per person
butter (don't substitute margarine)
I-2 cloves garlic, crushed (optional)

1 Clarify the butter by melting over a low heat. Allow it to cool slightly and skim off the scummy bits, leaving the clear butter. Add garlic if you like.
2 Place the cooked lobster on a serving dish, and remember to put out finger bowls. When you are ready to serve, heat the butter again, gently. Serve it in individual pots.
3 Break the lobster in two behind the head. Break off the tailpieces: you will find a hole at the base of the tail. Gently push up through this hole and you will find that the tail piece will slide out of its shell. Twist off the legs and claws – the large claws are full of good meat, so crack them carefully. Do not eat the stomach, the spongy gills, or the intestine, which looks like a vein running the length of the tail.
4 Dip the pieces of lobster meat in the clarified butter and eat. It is best served accompanied by nothing more elaborate than a simple green salad, and garnished with wedges of lemon.

New England boiled dinner

'This is a very traditional meal, a good family dish. Everything gets cooked in the same pot, so you have not only dinner but some very good stock to use for soup later. The recipe is sometimes accompanied by Harvard beets, in which case the root vegetables are served around the meat, but the cabbage is served with the beets. Mustards and horseradish are excellent condiments for this dish. It is also common to serve blueberry muffins with this meal. '

1 Place the beef in a saucepan and cover with water. Cover the pan and simmer for about 1½ hours. Skim off any scum appearing – if there is a lot you may prefer to change the water halfway through cooking.
2 Peel and quarter the root vegetables and add to the pan. Cook for another 20-30 minutes.
3 Quarter the cabbage and add to the pot. Cook for a further 10-15 minutes, or until the cabbage is cooked.
4 Remove the meat from the pan and place on a serving dish. Place the vegetables around it, reserving the stock for use in soup later.

New England rabbit stew

Serves: 4.
4 rabbit pieces
2 sticks celery, chopped
1 large onion, chopped
1 small green pepper, chopped
2 cloves garlic, crushed
2 tbsp oil
handful of fresh parsley, chopped
1-2 tsp salt
1 tsp black pepper
1 tsp oregano
3 tbsp tomato ketchup
about 300 ml/10 fl oz water

'This needs to cook fairly slowly, giving time for the liquor to reduce to a thick and delicious goo. The meat becomes mouthwateringly tender and not at all dry, and the sauce makes it special enough to serve to guests. '

1 Chop the celery, onion, and pepper. Crush the garlic and place all in a heavy-bottomed casserole dish or stew pan, with a lid. Add the oil, and the rabbit pieces and cook for about 10 minutes, turning the meat to brown. If your pan is not large enough to lay the meat more or less in a single layer, brown it in a large frying pan, and then transfer to the casserole dish.
2 Chop the parsley and add along with the other seasonings, the ketchup and water. Mix in, cover, and simmer for 2-3 hours.
Note: This dish can be made most successfully in a slow cooker, in which case allow 8-10 hours.
3 Serve hot, with the sauce spooned over the meat. It needs nothing fancier than plain boiled potatoes.

Boston baked beans

'Well, here we have one of the most famous of American dishes. The New England settlers are said to have learnt their ways with beans from the indigenous Indians. Certainly beans, along with molasses and fish, seem to be a hallmark of the cooking of this region. These beans take a long time a-cooking – they were commonly prepared on a Saturday and cooked slowly through the night, ready for Sunday's meal, thus keeping the strict Sabbath of the old settlers. This is a most substantial dish – rather sweet and lightly spicy, thick and very satisfying. '

Serves: 4-6.
450 g/1 lb dried haricot beans
1 medium onion, finely chopped
175 ml/6 fl oz reserved bean liquid
3 heaped tbsp molasses (regular, not blackstrap)
2 tbsp ketchup
3-4 tsp dry mustard powder
1 tsp salt
dash of cider vinegar
2 tsp curry powder
2 tbsp Worcester sauce
2 thick slices streaky bacon (or more, thinly sliced)

1 Soak the beans in cold water for several hours or overnight. Boil in fresh water for 30 minutes. Drain, reserving the liquid.
2 Chop the onion and place, with the beans, in a greased casserole dish (with a lid). You can also use a crockpot or slow cooker.
3 Measure out the reserved liquid and if you haven't enough, make up amount with water. Add to it the molasses, ketchup, and all other seasonings. Stir and pour over the beans. Place the slices of bacon on top of the beans.
4 Cover and bake at 120°C/250°F/Gas Mark ½ for 8-9 hours. Check every now and then, turning the beans so that those on top don't dry out. If, towards the end of cooking they have got too dry, add a dribble of water to moisten. The longer you bake them the darker the beans get. When they are soft, and a good rich brown, they are ready.

Right: Boston baked beans

Harvard beets

We are told that the name refers to the colour of the beets being that of the famous college, but this sounds a mite apocryphal! However it got its name, it's a delicious way of preparing beetroot – in a thickish sauce, slightly sweet, slightly sour.

Serves: 4-6 as a vegetable side dish.
4 medium-large beetroots, cooked (not in vinegar)
1 tbsp cornflour
115 g/4 oz white sugar
½ tsp salt
2 whole cloves
120 ml/4 fl oz cider vinegar

1 Peel the beetroots and either dice them coarsely or cut into 3-5 mm/⅛-¼ in slices.
2 In the top of a double boiler over hot water, simmering, cook the flour, sugar, salt and cloves with the vinegar, stirring until the mixture becomes clear.
3 Add the sliced beetroot, and cook for about 30 minutes. The slices should be well coated with the sauce, but be careful when stirring not to mash the beetroot.
4 Serve hot. It is an excellent accompaniment to fairly plainly cooked meat or fish, traditionally served with New England boiled dinner, and superb with Codfish hash (see recipes on pages 116 and 117).
Serving suggestion: Although it is perfectly possible to serve immediately, we suggest that you make it the day before. Leave the beetroot sitting in the sauce so the flavours really blend, and heat through gently just before serving. In fact, we had some left over and ate it a week later – it was even better!

Vermont scalloped parsnips

This is a most ample side dish – you may find it makes a very adequate supper dish. Soft, sweet parsnips, and the crisp, crunchy croutons with melted cheese topping make a lovely combination of tastes and contrasting textures – it looks most attractive too.

Serves: 4-6 as a side dish, 3-4 as a supper dish.
6 bacon rashers
3-4 parsnips, sliced fairly thickly
1-2 onions, sliced
1 tbsp fresh parsley, chopped
300 ml/10 fl oz milk
3 eggs
1 tsp salt
1 tsp black pepper
about 50 × 1 cm/½ in bread cubes or croutons, seasoned
115-175 g/4-6 oz Cheddar, grated

1 Fry or grill the bacon rashers until crisp. Leave to cool before crumbling into smallish pieces.
2 Slice the parsnips (peeled, or not, as you prefer) and onions fairly thickly, and chop the parsley.
3 Lightly grease a baking dish, and fill with alternate layers of parsnips, onions, and bacon, with sprinklings of parsley.
4 Mix the milk and the eggs, and season. Pour this over the vegetables. Top with a layer of the seasoned croutons/bread cubes, and a generous spread of grated cheese.
5 Cover and bake at 180°C/350°F/Gas Mark 4 for ¾-1 hour, until the parsnips are done. Uncover for the last 15 minutes or so, to let the top brown a little. Serve hot. It goes well with a fairly simple main course, and green vegetables.
Note: To make the croutons from scratch: take 3 large slices of bread (preferably brown, and not too fresh), cut about 1 cm/½ in thick. Season some butter with salt, pepper and whatever else you like to add, and lightly spread both sides of the bread. Remove the crusts, and cut the slices into 1 cm/½ in cubes, and place in a single layer in a baking tin or sheet at the bottom of the oven, set at the lowest temperature, for at least 2 hours. It's a good way to use up old bread, and gives you a handy stock which you can store in a screw-top or other airtight container, in the refrigerator. If you have no croutons, nor the time to make some, you could use breadcrumbs – please, *not* the orange manufactured kind!

Pumpkin pie

shortcrust pastry, to line baking pans
Filling:
400-425 g/14-15 oz pumpkin
3 eggs, lightly beaten
85 g/3 oz white sugar
85 g/3 oz brown sugar
½ tsp salt
2 tsp ground cinnamon
½-1 tsp ground ginger
½-1 tsp ground cloves
½-1 tsp allspice
1 × 385 g/13 oz can evaporated milk

‘The original pumpkin pie was a rather different dish, much loved by the Pilgrim Fathers. The pumpkin was hollowed out, filled with a mixture of milk, spices and honey, and baked until tender. But it is this spicy deep golden tart which is now traditionally served at Thanksgiving and Christmas, and any American who doesn't like it is banned from being a Yank! It's very much a taste you grow up with, so we don't promise you'll like it. We think canned pumpkin has a better taste, but you may use fresh if you prefer – cook it first. ,

1 Preheat the oven to 200°C/425°F/Gas Mark 6. Lightly grease a 23 cm/9 in deep pie pan or 2 × 20cm/8 in shallow flan tins. Prepare the shortcrust pastry shell.
2 In a mixing bowl, stir together the pumpkin (cooked), eggs and all the sugar.
3 Add all the seasonings and the evaporated milk. Mix well and pour into the pie shell.
4 Bake for 15 minutes at the high temperature. Reduce heat to 180°C/350°F/Gas Mark 4 and bake for another 45 minutes – less if you are doing 2 shallower pies.
5 Serve hot, warm, or cold, with whipped cream.

Blueberry pie

shortcrust pastry for double pie crust
Filling:
450-675 g/1-1½ lb berries
1½ tbsp lemon juice
2 tbsp cornflour or arrowroot
50 ml/2 fl oz water or juice from the fruit
175-225 g/6-8 oz white sugar
1-2 tbsp butter or margarine
a little milk to glaze

‘Blueberries, though not impossible to find, are not common here – try bilberries or whortleberries. This recipe may also be used for other fruit pies: blackcurrants, gooseberries, blackberries, raspberries, loganberries, or strawberries all work well. The amounts you need depend on the capacity of your pie dish. ,

1 Preheat the oven to 230°C/450°F/Gas Mark 8. Grease a 23 cm/9 in pie dish. Prepare the pastry and line the bottom of the dish.
2 Prepare the fruit: wash and drain, drying off as best you can. Add the lemon juice to the berries.
3 Mix the cornflour/arrowroot with water and blend to a paste. Add the sugar, and mix gently with the fruit. Let the mixture stand for 15 minutes before pouring it into the pie shell.
4 Dot the fruit with butter/margarine. Cover with the top crust (or cut pastry into strips to make a latticed top). Brush the pastry with milk to glaze.
5 Bake for 10 minutes, reduce the heat to 180°C/350°F/Gas Mark 4 and bake for a further 40-45 minutes.
6 Cool before serving – best eaten *à la mode* (with ice cream!).

*Right: Pumpkin pie,
Blueberry pie and
Philadelphia ice cream
(recipe, page 125)*

Apple pandowdy

'This is a homely baked dish – apple is usual, but you may use other fruit if you prefer. If you use dried fruit, omit the first baking. We make it in a dish the shape of a loaf tin – you need more depth than surface. **,**

Serves: 4.
2-3 fairly large Bramleys or other good cooking apples
50-85 g/2-3 oz sugar
dash of salt
½ tsp nutmeg, or to taste
½ tsp ground cinnamon or to taste
about 120 ml/4 fl oz water
Topping:
4 oz plain white flour
1½ tsp baking powder
½ tsp salt
25 g/1 oz butter or margarine
about 50 g/2 oz sugar
120 ml/4 fl oz milk

1 Preheat the oven to 220°C/425°F/Gas Mark 7. Peel and slice the apples, and lay them in the baking dish. Sprinkle on the sugar, salt and spices, and add the water. Bake, uncovered, for about 20 minutes.
2 Make the topping: sift the flour with the baking powder and salt, and cut or rub in the fat until you have grains (as you would for a crumble topping). Add the sugar (you can, of course, do this before but if using your hands to rub in, it's less gritty to add it later). If you prefer, you need not add the sugar at this stage, but simply sprinkle it on top of the dough just before you bake it.
3 Add the milk – you will have a very sloppy dough which is spooned over the fruit. Return to the oven and bake for 20-30 minutes. The top should be a pale golden brown.
4 Serve hot, with cream or ice cream.

Shoofly pie

'This is a traditional Pennsylvania Dutch dessert pie. We have two recipes for it: the one we give below has a richer (and boozier!) bottom layer. It's a delicious, sweet and very rich pie with flavours impossible to dissociate from Christmas – rum, raisins, sugar, pastry. **,**

shortcrust pastry to line flan tin
Filling:
115 g/4 oz raisins
50 g/2 oz dark brown sugar
¼ tsp bicarbonate of soda
2 tbsp rum
Toppings:
115 g/4 oz plain white flour
½ tsp ground cinnamon
½ tsp ground ginger
¼-½ tsp nutmeg, freshly grated if possible
50 g/2 oz butter or margarine
50 g/2 oz dark brown sugar

1 Place the raisins in a bowl with the sugar, bicarbonate of soda, and the rum. Cover and leave to soak for several hours or overnight.
2 Preheat the oven to 190°C/375°F/Gas Mark 5. Grease a 20 cm/8 in flan tin. Prepare the pastry shell.
3 Sift the flour with the spices, and rub in the fat.
4 Fill the pastry shell with the soaked raisins, spooning the thick rummy syrup into the shell. Spread the crumble-like topping over the raisins. Sprinkle a good layer of brown sugar over the crumble, covering completely. Bake for about 45 minutes.
5 Serve warm or cold, with cream – whipped or soured, either is good. Or try it with Philadelphia ice cream (see recipe on page 125) for a real sweet sensation!

Philadelphia ice cream

This is probably the simplest recipe for ice cream. It takes only a few minutes to make, and will set in the freezer compartment of a refrigerator.

Serves: 4, in small portions.
300 ml/10 fl oz single cream
50 g/2 oz caster sugar (or vanilla sugar if available)
½ tsp vanilla essence

1 Pour the cream into a heavy-bottomed pan, add the sugar, and heat gently, stirring until the sugar has melted.
2 Add the vanilla esence. Pour the cream into a container – such as a plastic storage container with a lid. Once the cream has cooled a little, cover and place in the freezer compartment for several hours or overnight. Allow it to thaw slightly before serving. All you have to do then is to sit back and enjoy the treat of *real* ice cream!

Boston cream pie

This famous 'pie' is actually a layered dessert cake, the success of which lies in getting each component right – a lovely light sponge with runny vanilla custard is awful, while a leathery or leaden sponge is even worse! It was very nearly our Waterloo, but we triumphed in the end! Since you, dear reader, are a superb cake-baker you should have no trouble.

Sponge:
4 or 5 eggs (depending on size)
175 g/6 oz caster sugar
175 g/6 oz plain flour
pinch of salt
40 g/1½ oz butter or margarine
4½ tbsp hot water
Custard filling:
115 g/4 oz caster sugar (vanilla sugar, if possible)
3 tbsp cornflour
450 ml/15 fl oz warm milk
4 egg yolks
1 tsp vanilla essence
Chocolate glaze:
150-175 g/5-6 oz plain chocolate (block or chips)
50 g/2 oz butter or margarine

1 Make the sponge: preheat the oven to 190°C/375°F/Gas Mark 5. Grease two 23 cm/9 in layer tins and dust with flour. For best effects, warm the bowls and tools first, and have all ingredients at room temperature.
2 Beat the eggs until they are fluffy and lighter in colour. Beat in the sugar vigorously until the mixture is thick.
3 Sift the flour with the salt, and gently fold into the egg mixture.
4 Melt the fat in hot water and fold into the mixture. Turn the mixture into the tins and bake for 25-30 minutes. Test by pressing lightly – when it is done the sponge should spring back.
5 Gently turn out and cool on a rack. The sponge must be *completely* cooled before sandwiching with the custard.
6 Make the custard filling: use a double boiler if you have one. Place hot water in the bottom and keep hot. For the first stage, use the top over direct heat: mix the sugar with the cornflour and add the milk, stirring until it boils. Boil for one minute.
7 Beat the egg yolks and add to them a little of the hot milk mixture. Stir, and combine the two.
8 Now place the top pan over the bottom so that the custard cooks over hot water. Stir until it thickens – about 5-10 minutes.
9 Add the vanilla, and leave to cool. You can place the top pan in a bowl of cold water, and stir the custard to help the release of steam. It also helps to prevent a skin forming. When it has cooled a little, place in the refrigerator to chill.
10 When both sponge and custard are thoroughly cold, sandwich together.
11 Make the chocolate glazing: melt the broken pieces of chocolate in the top of a double boiler, or over very gentle heat. Add the butter/margarine and stir until it is well mixed. Allow to cool slightly before spreading over the top of the sponge. Leave to set before serving.
Note: The original Boston cream pie was finished with a light dusting of icing sugar in place of the chocolate glazing, but this latter version is now more common – and very delicious!

Cinnamon rolls and pecan rolls

'These hail originally from Philadelphia and are otherwise known as Philadelphia sticky buns, or Cinnamon buns. We would probably call them buns too, rather than rolls, but whatever the name, they are delicious! Both types are made with the same dough and filling – the difference is in the frosting. In America they are eaten for breakfast or with morning coffee, and are a favourite item on the menu at the long-distance truckers' stops where they are served freshly made, hot, spicy, and hugely satisfying. '

Makes: 24. Halve the amounts for the dough, to make a smaller batch of 12.

Dough for 24 rolls:
4 level tsp dried yeast
225 ml/8 fl oz water
50 g/2 oz margarine, melted
6 tbsp sugar (granulated or caster)
1 tsp salt
2 eggs
450-550 g/1-1¼ lb plain white flour plus flour for rolling dough

Filling:
For each batch of 12:
1 tbsp margarine, melted
50-85 g/2-3 oz sugar
2 tsp cinnamon
2-3 handfuls of raisins

Frostings:
For Cinnamon rolls (12):
icing sugar
water

For Pecan Rolls (12):
50-85 g/2-3 oz pecan nuts, chopped (or walnuts)
115 g/4 oz brown sugar, light or dark
120 ml/4 fl oz corn or maple syrup (if unavailable, try a mixture of golden syrup and molasses)
25 g/1 oz butter or margarine, melted

1 Make the dough: dissolve the yeast in the water. Set the fat to melt. Stir into the yeast mixture the sugar, salt, and the melted butter. Add the eggs and begin to mix in the flour, a little at a time, until you have a soft dough.

2 Turn out the dough onto a lightly floured surface and knead for a minute or two until smooth. If making a full batch, divide the dough in half. Roll out the first batch into a rectangle about 45×23 cm/18×9 in.

3 Melt the tablespoon of fat for the filling. Brush the surface of the dough with it. Sprinkle with sugar, and with a liberal coating of ground cinnamon. Top with a layer of raisins.

4 Roll up the dough, beginning with a longer side, until you have a long sausage or Swiss roll shape. With a sharp knife cut into 12 pieces.

For Cinnamon rolls: 5 Lightly grease a shallow 20-23 cm/8-9in tin (a sandwich tin is ideal), and place the rolls, cut side down, around the tin and in the middle. As the dough rises, they will form a solid mass which can be pulled apart into individual rolls when cooked.

6 Cover and leave in a warm place to rise for about 30-45 minutes.

7 Place in the oven to bake – no real need to preheat – at 190°C/375°F/Gas Mark 5 for 30 minutes or so, until golden brown.

8 When cooked, remove from the oven. Immediately place a large plate over the pan, and turn out the circle of buns. Place another plate on top and turn back, so the rolls are once more right side up.

9 Mix icing sugar with hot water to make a fairly runny glacé icing, and dribble over the warm rolls. Leave to cool slightly, and serve still warm.

Serving suggestion: As a variation, don't ice, but simply serve with a knob of butter melting on top of each roll.

For Pecan rolls: 5 Chop the nuts fairly coarsely and set aside.

6 Mix the sugar, syrup, and the butter in a pan over gentle heat. Stir in the nuts and pour the mixture into a 20-23 cm/8-9 in sandwich layer tin.

7 Place the buns in the tin (as above), on top of the syrup. Cover and leave to rise for 30-45 minutes, in a warm place such as an airing cupboard. Bake as for cinnamon rolls.

8 When cooked, remove from the oven, and turn out by placing a plate over the buns and flipping them over. With these rolls there is no need to turn again, since these you want upside down, i.e., the syrup side uppermost.

9 Allow to cool a little – hot syrup is dangerously hot! Eat them warm, with a mug of steaming good coffee!

Right: Cinnamon rolls and pecan rolls

chapter

7.

The South

Where 'Country'
meets 'Soul'

*F*inally, *we come full circle, to the tradition-steeped South, where one is continually reminded of America's chequered history. You've probably read* Gone With the Wind, *or seen the film; heard of Abraham Lincoln and the Gettysburg Address, and the terrible Civil War . . . it all happened here in the South. As a Yank (an American from north of the Mason-Dixon Line) the South seems to me a country in itself. It's a region of contrasts: much of the wealth was derived from cotton and tobacco and some of the huge plantations still exist; in parts of both cities and rural areas, mansions with acres of gardens lie next to rows of shanty houses. The South has some beautiful cities – Atlanta, Georgia boasts some of the finest modern architecture. It's an area rich in diversity; the Atlantic and Gulf Coasts, the swamplands of Florida, Georgia – the famous Okefenokee – and South Carolina; the mountains of Alabama and Tennessee, the blue-grass country of Kentucky, renowned worldwide for its horsebreeding. With the exceptions of the moun-*

tains, of course, the climate is generally hot and humid, the winters mild – snow in South Carolina, Georgia or Florida is quite a rare event and tends to cause much chaos.

The ethnic heritage of the South is the most fascinating, and the food, as a result, probably the most 'American'. There is a very high proportion of blacks from whom comes a great influence in American cooking – 'soul food'. Here too the influence of the American Indian is perhaps most strong, with sweetcorn and cornmeal, beans, pecans, fish and game. The Cherokee nation occupied much of the South and many Southerners boast of having Indian blood. More recently, Cubans have moved to America, the highest concentration settling in Florida. Their culinary influence is not yet integrated, but I'm sure we'll soon have to include it in an update.

Georgia is known as The Peach State; it also has many peanut farms (remember President Carter's?), and you'll find recipes to match! We've tried to include a good many traditional dishes, and a few less so. It is good hunting and shooting country – possum, squirrel, duck, rabbit, raccoon – all would be stewed or fried (we've used alternative meats). Southerners like their food hot, and salty too. Cayenne is quite heavily used, and black pepper, but other herbs and spices are less popular. Corn-meal and buttermilk are common ingredients in Southern cooking and, when it comes to things sweet, they do mean sweet!

I must give credit to Grandma and Grandpa Martin from South Carolina for giving me some recipes for this chapter.

Now, get to know your distant cousins better by having a go at what they may be eating!

Southern corn soup

❝This is a thickened milk-based soup, with a rather delicate taste (though this depends a little on how much pepper you care to add!)

It can be made with fresh corn, the kernels stripped from the cob, but we have used tinned sweetcorn here. ❞

Serves: 4.

325 g/I × 11½ oz can sweetcorn (not the creamed variety)
600 ml/20 fl oz milk
I small onion, peeled, whole
I tbsp cornflour, mixed to a paste with a little cold water
½ tsp black pepper
salt to taste
knob of butter

1 Pour the milk into the saucepan and add the onion, seasoning, and heat gently until milk is simmering, but *do not boil.*
2 Drain the canned corn and add to the milk. (If using fresh, cut down through the middle of the kernels with a sharp knife and then scrape down the cob to extract the inner kernels.) Let the corn and milk simmer for 5 minutes (or a little longer if using fresh).
3 Mix the cornflour to a paste and add to the soup. Stir well and cook for a further 5 minutes.
4 Remove the onion, season to taste, and just before serving, add a knob of butter to the soup.

Peanut soup

❝Georgia is a great nut-producing area, and peanuts are used in many a dish. This is a rather unusual soup, and you really need a blender to make it well. ❞

Serves: 4.

I small onion
I small stick of celery
15 g/½ oz butter or margarine
2 tbsp plain flour
450 ml/15 fl oz chicken stock or 450 ml/15 fl oz water with I chicken stock cube
300 g/II oz wholefood peanut butter
2-3 tsp lemon juice
black pepper to taste

1 Finely chop the onion and celery, and sauté in the fat, but don't allow to burn.
2 Stir in the flour, and gradually add the stock. Cook gently for about 20 minutes.
3 Let the soup cool before thoroughly blending. Return to the pan, heat through and add the peanut butter. Stir until well mixed, and add the lemon juice and pepper.
4 Adjust the consistency – this will vary according to the peanut butter used. If you want to thin it, add a little water or milk.
5 Heat through gently and serve hot.

Grandpa Martin's vegetable soup

❝A very thick chunky soup using many of the commonly found Southern vegetables. Quick and easy to put together, this soup goes very well with cornbread. ❞

Serves: 4.

2 medium carrots, sliced
115 g/4 oz okra
2 medium potatoes, cut into 2.5 cm/I in cubes
225-350 g/8-12 oz lima beans (or broad beans or butter beans – fresh, frozen or canned)
I × 700 g/14 oz can tomatoes, with their juice
600 ml/20 fl oz water
115 g/4 oz salt pork or bacon
I tsp each salt, black pepper, cayenne

1 Prepare the vegetables – cut the tops off the okra and chop into cubes. Put all the vegetables into a large saucepan and add the tomatoes, juice, and water.
2 Slice the pork/bacon into 2.5 cm/I in pieces and add to the pot. Add the seasoning.
3 Bring to the boil, reduce heat, and simmer for about I hour.
4 Adjust the seasoning and serve hot.

Overleaf: Chicken pie with sweet potato crust (recipe, page 134) and Succotash (recipe, page 138)

Biscuits and red-eye gravy

This is a real Southern breakfast dish. The biscuits are similar to our scones, though a little flatter and slightly doughier; the gravy is very thick and quite spicy hot – the way Southerners like it! It's called red-eye because it is made with the bacon fat.

Serves: 4.
350-450 g/³⁄₄-1 lb back bacon or gammon slices
2 tbsp plain flour
up to 2 tbsp fat (see 4, below)
about 300 ml/10 fl oz water
1 tsp salt
1-2 tsp black pepper
4-6 dashes Tabasco sauce
Biscuits:
225 g/8 oz plain flour
3 tsp baking powder
1 tsp salt
3 tbsp vegetable shortening or margarine
175 ml/6 fl oz milk

1 Make the biscuit dough: mix the dry ingredients and cut in the fat. Add the milk, and stir until the dough holds together. On a lightly floured surface, knead for a minute or two, and roll out to 1 cm/½ in thick. Cut out the biscuits with a pastry cutter or upturned glass: a 6.5 cm/2½ in diameter cutter will give you about 10 biscuits.
2 Place on a baking sheet – they do not spread and will not rise much either. Bake at 220°C/425°F/ Gas Mark 7 for 12-15 minutes.
3 Meanwhile, fry the bacon/gammon. When cooked, remove, drain on absorbent paper, and keep warm. Reserve the fat.
4 Now make the sauce: you need about 2 tablespoons fat, so use the reserved bacon fat and if necessary add some vegetable shortening or margarine to make up the quantity. Over a gentle heat, mix in 2 tablespoons flour, and gradually add the water to make a really thick sauce.
5 Add the salt, pepper, and Tabasco, and let it simmer for a few minutes.
6 When the biscuits are done, fork them apart, spoon the gravy over, and serve with slices of bacon.
Note: Kenna's father-in-law says that the traditional way of making the gravy is to cook the ham, and remove it along with most of the fat, which you reserve. Then throw in yesterday's coffee grounds, add the reserved fat, and cook a few minutes before pouring it, hot, over the biscuits. We thought you'd prefer our version!

Indian corn stew

This is a thick and very tasty mixture, perhaps to use more like the meat part of a Shepherd's pie than a stew. But whatever it's name, it's very simple to do, and served with baked potatoes, and perhaps a side salad, it makes a very good family meal.

Serves: 4.
½-1 small green pepper, finely chopped
1 medium onion, finely chopped
25 g/1 oz butter
450 g/1 lb minced beef
1 × 300 g/11 oz can sweetcorn
2 × 275 g/10 oz cans condensed cream of tomato soup
2 tsp sugar
2 tsp black pepper
1 tsp salt
½ tsp Worcester sauce
2 tbsp flour mixed with 2 tbsp water

1 Chop the pepper and onion, and sauté in butter for a few minutes. Add the minced beef and allow to brown.
2 Add the corn (drained), the soup, sugar, pepper, salt, Worcester sauce and Tabasco. Mix well and simmer for 15 minutes.
3 Mix the flour and water to a paste, and stir into the meat mixture. Simmer for another 5 minutes or so, and serve hot.
Note: Southerners like it hot, and would use more Tabasco than we have. Adjust according to your taste.

Brunswick stew

‘This is a Tennessee dish which in bygone days would have been made with squirrel meat, but chicken, or sometimes rabbit, is more likely to be used now. It is a fairly light stew – the beans and corn make a nice change. ’

Serves: 4.
225 g/8 oz chicken, boned and diced (about 2 small breasts are sufficient)
1 medium onion, chopped
2 potatoes, diced (not too small)
1 × 275 g/10 oz can broad beans (the US cook would use lima beans)
1 × 300 g/11 oz can sweetcorn
1 × 400 g/14 oz can tomatoes
1 tsp Worcester sauce
1 tbsp tomato ketchup
1 tsp each salt and black pepper
1 tsp lemon juice
25 g/1 oz butter

1 Cut the chicken into pieces, and chop the onion. Place in a saucepan, cover with water, and simmer for about 30 minutes.
2 Chop the potatoes and add along with all the other ingredients. Give it a stir, and simmer for another hour. Serve hot.

Chicken pie with sweet potato crust

‘An unusual pie with a marvellous combination of tastes – chicken in a creamy sauce, bright with carrots and parsley, topped with a rich golden crust which has a sweetness that wonderfully complements the delicate taste of the chicken. ’

Serves: 4-6.
2-3 good-sized chicken breasts
2 large carrots, diced
2 small-medium onions (use pearl onions if you can get them – but not canned!)
1-2 tbsp fresh parsley, chopped
2 tbsp plain flour
1 tsp baking powder
1 tsp salt
1 tsp black pepper
225 ml/8 fl oz milk
Crust:
4 medium sweet potatoes
about 225 g/8 oz plain flour
1-2 eggs
about 85 g/3 oz butter, melted

1 Preheat the oven to 180°C/350°F/Gas Mark 4. Lightly grease a baking dish or casserole.
2 Boil the chicken pieces in water to cover (at least 300 ml/10 fl oz). Cook until tender, remove the meat and allow to cool. Reserve the broth.
3 Dice the carrots, slice the onions and boil in water until tender. Drain. You can add them to the chicken as it cooks, to make a nicely enriched stock, if you prefer.
4 Boil the sweet potatoes, whole, in water, until soft and mashable. Drain and cool.
5 Chop the parsley. Skin and dice the chicken and arrange, with the carrots, onions and parsley in the baking dish.
6 Mix together the flour, baking powder, salt and pepper, and slowly add the milk and an equal quantity of the reserved chicken stock. Stir well and pour over the chicken and vegetables.
7 Make the crust: mash the sweet potatoes (removing skins if you prefer). Mix in about 225 g/8 oz flour, and 1-2 eggs, lightly beaten (add one first – use another if you think the mixture is too dry). Add the melted butter. Mix well. The dough is of a fairly loose consistency (more like mashed potato than pastry). Spoon the mixture on top of the chicken, covering well.
8 Bake, uncovered, for about 45 minutes. Serve hot, with green vegetables, as the sweet potato crust is not, we think, too delicious when cold.

Right: Southern fried chicken (recipe, page 137), Hopping John (recipe, page 137) and Cornbread (recipe, page 145)

The South

Southern fried fish

> 6Use any white fish that is good for frying (but avoid flat fish). 9

Serves: 4.
4 fish pieces
oil for frying (depth about 1 cm/½ in)
Coating:
115-150 g/4-5 oz cornmeal
salt and pepper to season the cornmeal
about 150 ml/5 fl oz buttermilk

1 Mix the cornmeal with salt and pepper to season. Empty the buttermilk into a bowl and heat the oil in a frying pan.
2 Dip the cleaned and dried fish in the buttermilk, and roll in the seasoned cornmeal to coat. Repeat if necessary.
3 Fry in oil, turning once, until the fish is cooked through, and the coating crisp.
4 Drain on absorbent paper, and serve (traditionally, with hushpuppies – see recipe on page 140).

Catfish stew

> 6It is difficult to get an exact substitute for this unique indigenous fish (and Southern catfish is *not* the same fish that occasionally goes by that name here) but we've used huss, a good white fish which responds well to this treatment. It has a large and easily removable backbone (in fact, we just leave it – when the fish is cooked it will fall off the bone anyway) and no other nasty little bones. This is a spicy hot stew – very tasty! 9

Serves: 4.
4 pieces huss (serving portions)
4-6 slices streaky bacon
3 large onions, sliced
1 small green pepper
4 medium potatoes
4 tbsp concentrated tomato purée
300 ml/10 fl oz water
2-4 small dried red hot chilli peppers
2 bay leaves
1-2 tsp salt
1-2 tsp black pepper
2 tsp Tabasco sauce

1 Use a heavy-bottomed, lidded pan which will hold everything: cut the bacon slices in half, and cook them in the pan, sweating out as much fat as possible.
2 Meanwhile, slice the onions, green pepper, and potatoes fairly thinly.
3 When the bacon is done, remove, and place in the pan a layer of onions, then some bacon, 2 pieces of fish, some peppers, a layer of potatoes, another layer of onions, etc., ending with the top layer of potatoes. If you leave the bacon in the bottom of the pan, layering all else on top, you will end up with rather unappetizingly black pieces!
4 Mix the tomato purée in the water and add to the casserole. Add the chilli peppers and all other seasonings.
5 Cover, and simmer on medium heat for about 45 minutes, until the fish is well done.
6 Serve hot, with some good bread, or biscuits (see recipe for Biscuits and red-eye gravy on page 133) to soak up the gravy.

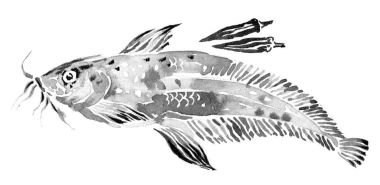

Southern fried chicken

A similar process to Southern Fried Fish (see opposite), but a different coating mix!

Serves: 4.
4 chicken pieces, skinned
oil for frying
coriander to garnish
Coating:
4-5 tbsp plain white flour
salt and pepper to season flour
I egg
2 tbsp milk

1 Halve the joints of chicken if you prefer. Have the seasoned flour in a bowl. In another, mix the egg and milk.
2 Roll the chicken pieces in flour, dip in the egg mixture, and roll in flour again until well covered. If necessary, repeat the process.
3 Fry the chicken – if the oil is not hot enough the chicken will shed its coating. Cook until richly golden all over, turning once.
4 Drain on absorbent paper and serve. Eat hot or cold. Garnish with coriander.

Hopping John (Black-eyed peas and rice)

This is a simple, warming dish, wholesome and filling – eating it on New Year's Eve is said to ensure good fortune for the coming year. Some claim that the name 'Hopping John' derives from a custom of children having to hop once around the table before being served. Others say it is named after a particularly lively waiter. We prefer the first version! Note that the famous black-eyed peas are called beans over here.

Serves: 4-6.
450 g/I lb dried black-eyed beans, soaked overnight
225 g/8 oz bacon or ham, cut into 2.5 cm/I in chunks
I-2 tsp salt
I tsp sugar
I tsp black pepper
USA long-grain rice for 4-6 servings

1 Drain the soaked beans and place in a saucepan. Pour in water to a level 2.5 cm/I in above the beans. Add the pieces of meat, and all the seasonings. Cook for 1-2 hours, simmering gently until the meat is cooked and the beans are soft. This is not a richly seasoned dish – you may like to add your favourite herbs.
2 Mash a few of the beans against the side of the pan (or if you prefer, remove and purée in a blender). Stir the mashed beans into the rest to thicken. Adjust seasoning.
3 Serve over boiled rice.

Succotash

Serves: 6.

1 × 450 g/1 lb can sweetcorn
1 × 450 g/1 lb can lima beans (or broad beans or butter beans)
25 g/1 oz butter or margarine
dash of salt
1-1½ tsp black pepper
½ tsp paprika
handful of fresh parsley, chopped (don't use dried)
2 tbsp sour cream

This was originally a native American Indian dish, and its name is a corruption of the Indian name 'misickquatash'. It is a very simple vegetable side dish, but quite delicious – the sour cream adds a dash of something different.

1 Drain the corn and the beans, and place in a saucepan with butter, salt, pepper, and paprika. Heat gently.
2 Chop the parsley and add to the beans.
3 When the butter/margarine has melted and it has all heated through, stir in the sour cream. Adjust the seasoning and serve hot.
Note: Lima beans are difficult to come by here, although you sometimes find them in the larger supermarkets. They are a member of the broad bean family, so broad beans or butter beans are just as good. Exact proportions don't matter, so don't worry if you find only 275 g/10 oz cans.

Collard greens

Serves: 4.

450 g/1 lb spring greens (stripped from the stalks, gives about 225 g/8 oz)
115-175 g/4-6 oz bacon, salt pork or gammon pieces
1 onion, chopped
2 tbsp vinegar, preferably cider (not malt)
2 tsp black pepper
about 6 dashes Tabasco sauce (optional)

Collard greens are what we call spring greens – they tend to be rather bitter, but this method of cooking them reduces the bitterness without rendering them too vinegary. In the States, turnip greens are also cooked this way. Try them if you can get hold of any.

1 Strip the leaves from their stalks, rinse, drain, and chop coarsely.
2 Chop the meat, and onion, and place in a saucepan with the greens. Add water to the depth of about 2.5 cm/1 in. Add the vinegar and seasoning.
3 Cover and cook for about 30 minutes over a low heat. Serve hot.

Okra in cornmeal

Serves: 2-4.

115-225 g/4-8 oz okra (depending on size)
3-4 tbsp plain flour
salt and black pepper to taste
1 egg
2 tbsp milk
3-4 tbsp cornmeal
oil for deep frying (depth about 1 cm/½ in)

This is a very common method of preparing okra, and also eggplant (aubergine), and is eaten with Southern fried chicken or fish.

1 Top and tail the okra – if they are very large you may prefer to cut them into smaller chunks.
2 In one bowl put the flour, seasoned with salt and pepper; in another, mix the egg and milk; in a third, the cornmeal, also seasoned with salt and pepper.
3 Heat the oil.
4 Dip each okra first in the flour, then in the egg, and then roll in cornmeal: it should have a thick coat. Lay in the hot fat and fry, turning once, for 3-4 minutes until crisp and golden.
5 Remove and drain on absorbent paper. Serve hot.

Right: Peach cobbler (recipe, page 141)

Hushpuppies

❝These are golden nuggets of crispy, crunchy deepfried cornmeal eaten with fried fish. It is said that the name derives from pioneer days when the travellers or hunters would make these over the camp fire, throwing some to the dogs to keep them quiet. ❞

Makes: about 24.
350 g/12 oz cornmeal
1 tsp baking powder
1 tbsp sugar
1 medium onion, finely chopped
1 egg
about 225 ml/8 fl oz milk
oil for deep frying (depth about 1 cm/½ in)

1 In a bowl mix the cornmeal, baking powder and sugar. Finely chop the onion and add to the cornmeal.
2 Beat together the egg and milk, and stir into the cornmeal, mixing well.
3 Heat the oil. Mould the cornmeal into small balls, about dessertspoon size, and drop into the hot oil. Fry a few at a time – if the oil is not hot enough, the balls will disintegrate. Cook both sides until light golden brown, remove and drain on absorbent paper. Serve hot.

Corn fritters

❝Also known as corn oysters, these are eaten as a vegetable accompaniment to chicken or fish, and may also feature on a Southerner's breakfast menu. ❞

Makes: about 15.
1 × 275 g/10 oz can sweetcorn, well drained
2 eggs, separated
85 g/3 oz plain flour
½ tsp baking powder
dash of salt
dash of nutmeg
oil for deep frying (depth about 1 cm/½ in)

1 Place the drained corn in a mixing bowl. Separate the eggs and add the yolks to the corn. Stir in the flour, baking powder, salt and nutmeg.
2 Beat the egg whites until they form soft peaks. Fold in the corn mixture.
3 Heat the oil. Gently drop tablespoonfuls of the corn mixture into the oil, a few at a time. When lightly golden, turn once and cook the other side.
4 Remove and drain on absorbent paper. Serve hot.
Note: Because the eggs are separated the batter is very light so these are not as heavy as they might otherwise be. When eaten for breakfast it is usual to dribble a little maple syrup on the fritters – it may sound quite awful but it's actually excellent.

Peach cobbler

> Yummm . . . a real 'pud' – hot, gooey, sweet, but not too heavy. Georgia is known as The Peach State and this is a local favourite.

Serves: 4, generously.
1.25 kg/2½ lb fresh peaches or nectarines (or equivalent, canned)
115 g/4 oz butter or margarine
115 g/4 oz plain white flour
2 tsp baking powder
225 g/8 oz white sugar
225 ml/8 fl oz milk

1 Preheat the oven to 180°C/350°F/Gas Mark 4.
2 Peel, stone and slice the peaches/nectarines and stew gently in a little water, to soften. If using canned fruit, just drain well.
3 Melt the butter/margarine and leave to cool a little.
4 Mix the dry ingredients with the cooled butter, and stir in the milk. Pour this batter into a baking dish (non-stick or lightly greased).
5 Lay the fruit slices in the batter. Don't worry if they are not well covered – the batter will rise over the fruit as it bakes.
6 Bake for 30-40 minutes. Serve hot.

Key lime pie

> Named after the region of Florida known as The Keys, this is a deliciously light dessert – perfect to follow a heavy meal. It has a crunchy base, and a featherlight filling with a pleasingly refreshing taste, the limes being both sweet and slightly tart.

Biscuit base:
225-275 g/8-10 oz digestive buscuits, crushed
85-115 g/3-4 oz butter or margarine
Filling:
120 ml/4 fl oz lime juice (juice of 4-5 limes)
grated rind of 1 lime
6 eggs, separated
225 g/8 oz caster sugar plus 2 tbsp
1 sachet gelatine, dissolved in 2-4 tbsp water

1 Make the biscuit base: crush the biscuits, melt the butter/margarine, mix together and pat into a 23 cm/9 in or 25 cm/10 in pie dish to form the base and sides of a shell.
2 Extract the juice from the limes and grate the rind of one (or use a zester, which ensures that you remove none of the pith).
3 Separate the eggs – you need 6 yolks but only 4 whites. Beat the yolks gradually adding the sugar, and very slowly, mix in the lime juice and the rind.
4 Dissolve the gelatine as per packet directions, and beat into the egg mixture. Place in the refrigerator to chill while you tackle the next step.
5 Beat the 4 egg whites to stiff peaks, and whisk in 2 tablespoons caster sugar. Beat until the mixture is thick and glossy. (If you don't get the egg whites stiff enough the filling will be a bit on the runny side – it won't look so good, but it will still taste divine.) Then fold in the chilled egg mixture, and pour into the biscuit shell. Return to the refrigerator to chill for several hours before serving.

Pecan pie

115-175 g/4-6 oz pecans, coarsely chopped
85 g/3 oz butter
150 g/5 oz dark brown sugar
4 eggs
shortcrust pastry to line pie dish
225 ml/8 fl oz corn syrup or molasses (regular, not blackstrap)
2 tsp vanilla essence or 1 tbsp white rum
½ tsp salt

1 Use a 23 cm/9 in pie dish or halve the amounts (use 50 g/2 oz butter) to make filling for a 20 cm/8 in flan tin. Prepare the pastry shell. Preheat the oven to 230°C/450°F/Gas Mark 8.
2 Cream the butter and the sugar. Add the eggs, one at a time, and beat well.
3 Chop the nuts and add to the mixture. Stir in the syrup/molasses, and the vanilla essence/rum, and the salt. Mix well.
4 Pour into the pie shell and bake for 30 minutes.
5 Serve warm, or cold, with whipped cream.

Carrot cake

'If you've never before tried a carrot cake, do take the plunge. It's a moist, sweet, slightly spiced cake, which is very popular in the States, where it is commonly served as a dessert cake, for dinners or buffets and barbecues. '

6 large carrots, shredded
50-115 g/2-4 oz walnuts or pecan nuts, chopped
4 eggs
350 ml/12 fl oz light vegetable oil
450 g/1 lb granulated sugar
225 g/8 oz plain flour
2 tsp baking powder
2 tsp ground cinnamon
1 tsp ground cloves
1 tsp ground ginger
1 tsp allspice

1 Preheat the oven to 180°C/350°F/Gas Mark 4, and lightly grease a 25 cm/10 in ring mould or equivalent tin.
2 Shred or grate the carrots, and chop the nuts.
3 In a mixing bowl beat the eggs, oil, and sugar, and add the carrots.
4 Mix in the flour and all the other dry ingredients. Mix well, pour into the pan, and bake for 45 minutes.
5 Allow to cool before turning out, then ice with Cream cheese frosting (see recipe below).

Cream cheese frosting

'This is a very popular cake frosting commonly used for Carrot cake, Red velvet cake, and Applesauce cake. It is very simple to make, and gives the perfect finishing touch. '

Makes: enough to frost a 23 cm/9 in layer cake.
225 g/8 oz cream cheese
115 g/4 oz margarine
350-400 g/12-14 oz icing sugar
1 tsp vanilla essence

1 Melt the cream cheese and margarine together over low heat, and let the mixture cool a little.
2 Sift the icing sugar (it avoids lumps and the subsequent hard work to get rid of them) and beat it into the cheese mixture. Use about 350 g/12 oz at first. Add the vanilla and mix well.
3 Leave the frosting to cool and check consistency: it should be thick but spreadable. You may need to add more icing sugar – perhaps another 50 g/2 oz.
4 Spread the frosting over the top and sides of the cake, or in between layers.

Left: Carrot cake

Red velvet cake

A good dessert cake – it has a rich red colour and a rich chocolate taste. It's also picturesquely known as Red devil cake. ,

2 eggs
350 g/12 oz granulated sugar
350 ml/12 fl oz light vegetable oil
1 tsp vinegar
275 g/10 oz plain flour
1 tsp bicarbonate of soda
dash of salt
225 ml/8 fl oz buttermilk
1½-2 tbsp cochineal or red food colouring
4 tbsp cocoa
1 tsp vanilla essence

1 Preheat the oven to 180°C/350°F/Gas Mark 4 and lightly grease and flour a 23 cm/9 in ring mould (or a round tin if you prefer).
2 Beat the eggs, and add the sugar, oil, and vinegar, and stir well.
3 Sift in the flour, bicarbonate of soda, and salt. Gradually add the buttermilk, and mix well.
4 Add the colouring – this seems a vast amount, but you are aiming for a rich dark red, so to colour with the cocoa, you do need lots.
5 Add the cocoa and the vanilla. Beat well, and pour into the tin. Bake for about 40 minutes. It rises a lot – test with a fork or skewer. This will come out clean when the cake is done.
6 Leave to cool a little before turning out. When the cake has cooled ice it with Cream cheese frosting (see recipe on page 143). If you have baked it in a round tin, it would be usual to split the cake into two or three layers – you then frost between the layers, and on top too, if you like.

Aunt Lee's plain cake (easy pound cake)

As I understand it, pound cakes were so called because they were made of one pound of each of the main ingredients. This one isn't, but it has a similar taste and texture. It's quite a heavy and moist cake, especially good served with homemade ice cream. ,

225 g/8 oz butter
450 g/1 lb icing sugar
4 eggs
350 g/12 oz plain flour
1 tsp baking powder
dash of salt
225 ml/8 fl oz milk
1 tbsp lemon or almond flavouring

1 Preheat the oven to 180°C/350°F/Gas Mark 4, and lightly grease and flour a 25 cm/10 in ring mould or equivalent square tin.
2 Cream the butter with the sugar (sifted first to get rid of lumps), and beat in the eggs, adding them one at a time.
3 Sift together the flour, baking powder and salt. Now add to the cake mixture a little milk, and then a little flour. Alternating, gradually add the rest of the milk and the flour. Stir in the lemon or almond flavouring.
4 Pour into the ring mould or tin. Place this in another larger, shallow pan, with water to about 2.5 cm/1 in depth. Place in the oven and bake for 1½ hours.
5 Leave to cool a little before turning out.

Cornbread

225 g/8 oz cornmeal (yellow or white, also called polenta)
115 g/4 oz plain white flour
3 tsp baking powder
2 tbsp granulated sugar
¾ tsp salt
25 g/1 oz margarine, melted
1 egg
225 ml/8 fl oz milk

This is a crumbly, almost cake-like bread, slightly grainy and slightly sweet. It is one of the easiest breads to make, and very quick.

1 Preheat the oven to 220°C/425°F/Gas Mark 7, and grease a 900 g/2 lb loaf tin or a 23 cm/9 in square tin. (The bread will rise a little, but nowhere near as much as yeasted bread).
2 In a bowl, mix all the dry ingredients.
3 Melt the margarine. Add the egg and milk to the dry ingredients along with the melted fat, and mix well. If it's very thick, add a little more milk. Pour into the tin and bake for 30 minutes or so, until the top is firm, and lightly golden brown.
4 Serve hot, with butter. To reheat, wrap in foil and place in the oven for a few minutes.

Georgia nut bread

Makes: one 550 g/1¼ lb loaf. Double the quantities if you want a larger one.
115 g/4 oz peanuts, finely chopped
1 egg
85 g/3 oz dark brown sugar
225 g/8 oz plain white flour
2 tsp baking powder
½ tsp salt
225 ml/8 fl oz milk

Very simple to make, this is a slightly sweet, non-yeast bread with a good, heavy cake-like texture – just the thing for tea.

1 Beat together the egg and the sugar. (If the sugar is very lumpy, sift if first.)
2 Sift together the flour, baking powder and salt, and stir into the egg mixture alternately with the milk.
3 Chop or coarsely grind the nuts and stir into the bread mixture. Pour into a well-oiled loaf tin, and let it stand for 30 minutes before baking.
4 Heat the oven to 180°C/350°F/Gas Mark 4, and bake for about 45-50 minutes. It will rise a little. Remove from the tin and cool on a rack.
5 Serve warm or cold. It's good enough to eat just as it comes, but you may prefer to serve it with butter, and cottage or cream cheese makes a tasty change.

145

8.

Across the Board

National Dishes

*L*ast but not least, here are those recipes which are truly American but seem to have no particular home. You know of, and have almost certainly eaten, hamburgers and Sloppy Joes, Brownies, Pizza American-style – all the sorts of dishes that turn up at a true American barbecue, or at our traditional Thanksgiving Dinner. Recipes for cocktails and other drinks are included in this section because although some have regional origins, they are served all over the United States.

Thanksgiving is a national holiday in the United States, a celebration to commemorate the pilgrims' survival of their first year in their new-found land, with provisions enough to see them through the winter. It is held each year on the fourth Thursday of November and very often stretches to a four-day weekend, since many take the opportunity of making it a big family festival – in many ways it is more celebrated than Christmas. The celebration centres on the Thanksgiving Dinner and just as here with Christmas Dinner, so in the States, the traditional fare varies according to the region. Of course every family has its own favourite dishes, although the basis is still the turkey, and other food indigenous to the north-east. Almost everywhere, the turkey is roasted, and then stuffed (the stuffings vary – we've given three recipes), and served with cranberries in some form or other, sometimes in jelly, or as a relish (try our New England recipe); others cook the berries whole, with orange juice and spices. There is a wide choice of side dishes: candied or glazed sweet potatoes or yams are very common, and mashed potatoes are often served, with other vegetables – corn on the cob is popular too – and of course, the turkey gravy. A fruit or jello salad is a common accompaniment, and the meal usually ends with pumpkin pie, topped with whipped cream or ice cream.

It's been a lot of fun, this cooking trip coast to coast, seaboard to seaboard across the United States: a great nostalgia trip for me, and a voyage of discovery for my English partner, now hooked on cornbread, hash browns, jalapeno bean dip, and Creole cooking. Quite the hardest aspect has been deciding what to leave out – we could do it all again and not repeat a single recipe! We've learnt a lot about food, and cooking; we've practically come to blows over terminology – who ever said we speak the same language?! – but we're still speaking, cooking, and eating, happily sharing food together, surely one of the greatest delights life has to offer.

We hope it's whetted your appetite, and we wish you all many shared meals, and the attendant shared enjoyment.

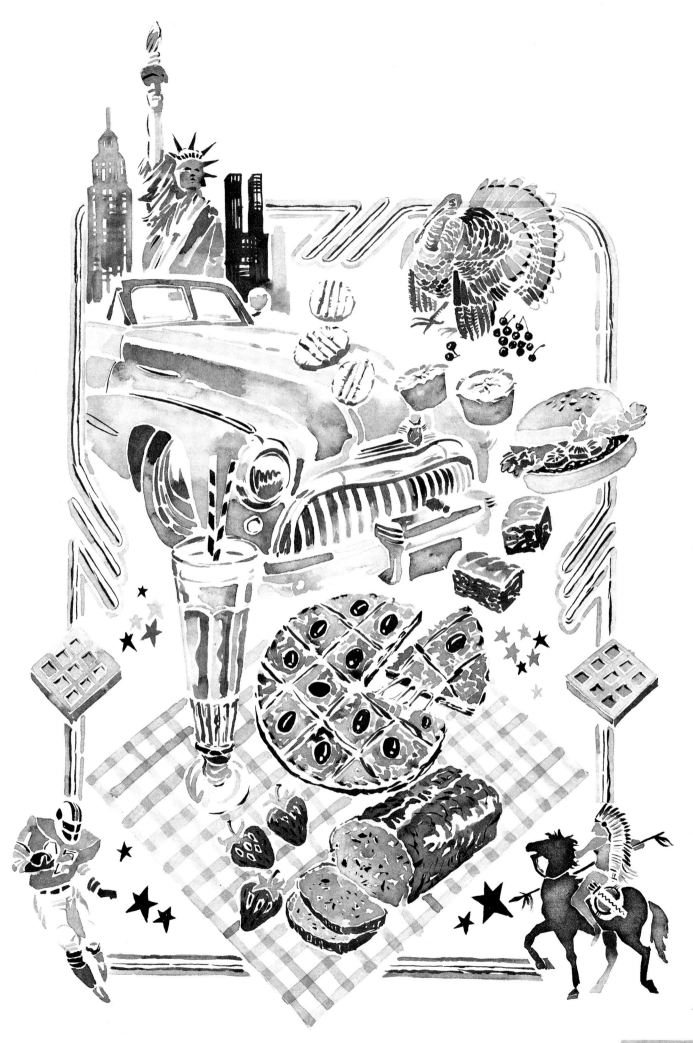

Waffles

'Waffles turn up on breakfast menus in coffee and pancake houses across the States. They are served with a wide variety of sweet toppings, the Bifani family favourite being fresh strawberries with dollops of whipped cream. '

Makes: 6 double squares.
3 eggs, separated
50 g/2 oz butter, melted
350 ml/12 fl oz milk
200 g/7 oz plain white flour
2 tsp baking powder
½ tsp salt
I tbsp sugar

1 Heat the waffle iron – it must be really hot, and very well oiled.
2 Separate the eggs. Whisk the whites until they are stiff.
3 Beat the yolks with the butter and milk, and fold in the dry ingredients.
4 Fold in the whites and spoon the batter into the waffle iron. How much to use at one time will be largely a matter of trial and error.
5 Cook until golden brown and as crisp as you like. Serve hot, with fresh fruit and cream, with maple or blueberry syrup. Jams are good too – or just sprinkle with sugar and lemon juice (not the American way but very tasty!).

Chipped beef on toast

'Chipped beef is made with wafer-thin slices of dried beef, pulled apart into small pieces and served in a creamy seasoned sauce, on toast. It's a popular breakfast or snack meal. Since we cannot find the exact meat, we have substituted slices of cooked cured brisket – it has a very similar taste though slightly moister texture. '

Serves: 4.
50-115 g/2-4 oz cooked cured brisket
65 g/1½ oz butter
I medium onion, finely chopped
3 tbsp plain flour
300 ml/10 fl oz milk
2-3 tbsp sherry (dry)
I tsp paprika
seasonings of your choice (watch the salt) – we suggest fresh parsley, black pepper, and chives
bread for toast

1 Chop and pull apart the beef slices. You want fairly small pieces. The amount of meat you use is really up to you but this is a topping in which there is more sauce than meat.
2 Chop the onion, and sauté gently in the butter, until softened and lightly browned.
3 Add the flour to the onions, stirring it in. Gradually add the milk, stirring until you have a smooth sauce. Add the beef.
4 Add the sherry, paprika and the other seasonings.
5 Make the toast, and serve, with chipped beef spooned on top.

Hash browns

These are eaten for breakfast in just about every area in the States, except in the South, where they prefer to have grits with their ham and eggs. Basically, it's fried potato, but it's so good!

Serves: 4.
8 medium potatoes, thinly sliced
1-2 onions, sliced
2 cloves garlic, crushed
1 tsp salt
2 tsp black pepper
2 tbsp oil for frying

1 Scrub and slice the potatoes – it is not necessary to peel them. Slice the onions. Lay them all in a large frying pan, with the garlic, and seasoning. Add the oil.
2 Cover and cook for about 30 minutes, turning the potato layers every so often until they are soft, with browned and crispy bits. Serve hot.
Note: There are many ways of preparing Hash browns: the potatoes may be diced very small, or grated raw, rather than sliced. You can, of course, use already cooked potatoes, or parboil if you want to cut down the cooking time. Any way, they are very tasty. If you think that onions and garlic may be a mite antisocial for breakfast, just leave them out.

Hoagies

While Hoagie is a fairly general name, in New Orleans these are Po' Boys, while Californians know them as Submarines; but whatever they are called, the basic item is a hearty sandwich – not the most graceful of its kind, but just one will suffice for a meal.

Makes: 4.
1 French loaf (baguette/yardstick) or 4 French rolls
12 slices salami
4-8 thin slices ham
4 slices luncheon meat or other cold meat
4 thin slices Cheddar
4 thin slices Gruyere or Emmenthal cheese
2 tomatoes, sliced into rings
1 onion, very thinly sliced into rings
4 large lettuce leaves
'American' yellow mustard (you can substitue 'German', but not 'English' – it's too strong)
mayonnaise (optional)
pickled dill cucumbers, sliced (optional)
jalapeno peppers, chopped (optional, but authentic for a New Orleans Po' Boy)

1 Slice the loaf in half lengthwise, and then cut the whole load into 4 equal portions. If using rolls, halve them.
2 Prepare all the fillings. Spread each cut side of the bread with mustard, and then (if you like) a layer of mayonnaise. (If you want a true American Hoagie, don't use any butter – as a rule, Yanks don't butter their sandwiches.)
3 Now add the rest in layers: the meats, cheeses, lettuce, tomato, onion, and then the dill cucumbers or the jalapeno peppers. Close the sandwich – and get your teeth around that!

Mock oyster dip

We've no idea why it's called Mock oyster, but never mind – it's a wonderful invention! You need to have a fondue pot or suchlike to serve it in, because the dip must be kept warm.

Serves: about 25 as party food.
2 medium onions, fairly finely chopped
225 g/8 oz butter or margarine
450 g/1 lb broccoli (fresh or frozen)
2 × 275 g/10 oz cans condensed cream of mushroom soup
225 g/8 oz mushrooms, chopped
450 g/1 lb Cheddar, grated or Cheddar cheese spread
Tabasco sauce to taste

1 Chop the onions and sauté in the butter (use a saucepan large enough to hold all the ingredients).
2 Cook the broccoli until tender, drain well, and chop into small pieces. Chop the mushrooms. Grate the cheese.
3 Add the mushrooms to the onions, and stir in the soup. Add all the other ingredients and simmer gently, stirring, until the cheese has melted and you have a thick and blended dip. Season with a dash or three of Tabasco.
4 Serve in a fondue pot, with crackers or corn chips.

Vegetable dip

This one is for, not of, vegetables! It has a rather strong taste which is a good foil for raw vegetable sticks – we use carrots, spring onions, celery, green pepper, cucumber, cauliflower – choose whatever you like.

Makes: about 600 ml/20 fl oz.
450 g/1 lb cream cheese
4-5 tbsp mayonnaise (homemade or bought)
2 beef stock cubes dissolved in about 150 ml/5 fl oz warm water
2 cloves garlic, crushed
½ small onion, finely chopped
black pepper
Garnish:
chopped parsley
paprika

1 Mix the cheese with the mayonnaise until smooth. Dissolve the stock cubes and add to the cheese mixture.
2 Add all the other ingredients. If you think the mixture too firm, loosen with a little water. It should be fairly thick, not runny. Chill.
3 Serve garnished with chopped parsley and a light sprinkling of paprika if liked.

Tuna mould

A good and easy dish for parties. Mould it into any shape you like, serve it in a bowl, have it as a side dish, or use as a spread.

Serves: about 10 as party food.
about 675 g/1½ lb canned tuna, drained well, and flaked
450 g/1 lb cream cheese
10-12 black olives, pitted and finely chopped
2 tbsp capers (optional)
50-115 g/2-4 oz walnuts or pecans, chopped
¼ tsp salt
¼ tsp black pepper
1½ tsp dry mustard
1 tsp thyme (or your favourite herb)

1 Drain and flake the tuna, and mash with the softened cream cheese.
2 Mix in the olives, capers and nuts. Add the seasoning, mix well, and refrigerate for at least 2 hours if you wish to mould the pâté into a fancy shape. Otherwise, turn out into a serving bowl, and chill.
3 When firm, mould into a shape.

Left: Waffles (recipe, page 148)

Hamburgers

You may think it crazy to give a recipe for hamburgers when they can so easily be bought in every supermarket, but they are not difficult to make – similar to making a meatloaf – and they do have that bit extra flavour. It really does make for a better barbecue burger – even if you use a lesser grade mince.

Makes: 8.
900 g/2 lb minced beef
50 g/2 oz dried breadcrumbs
I egg
I small onion, finely chopped
2-3 cloves garlic, crushed
I tsp Worcester sauce
salt and pepper to taste
8 bread buns

1 In a large bowl, mix together all the ingredients. Use your fingers to get them really well mixed.
2 Divide into 8 equal portions and form each into a patty the size of your buns.
3 Barbecue on a grill and serve in a bun or just as it comes, with the usual garnishes – onion rings, green salad, tomatoes, relishes. For side dishes you have a wide choice: coleslaws, baked potatoes, barbecued beans, all manner of salads, potato, jello, and others: French-fried onion rings, corn, . . . the list is almost endless!

Sloppy Joes

Sloppy Joes are minced beef cooked in a barbecue sauce, and eaten on burger buns – split the bun, ladle the meat stew on top, and eat. It's not elegant, but who cares?

Makes: 4-6. Treble the quantities for party food.
450 g/I lb minced beef
I large onion, chopped
I stick celery, chopped
I small green pepper, chopped
115 g/4 oz mushrooms, sliced or chopped
50 g/2 oz tomato ketchup
475 ml/16 fl oz tomato juice
2 tsp chilli seasoning
1-2 tsp salt
I tsp black pepper
2 tbsp tapioca

1 Put the meat into a pan, to brown. (Don't add any fat.) Chop the vegetables and add to the meat. Cook until they are tender.
2 Add the ketchup and the tomato juice. Add the seasoning, and mix in the tapioca, which acts as a thickening agent. Mix well, and cook on a very low heat for a minimum of two hours, but the longer the better. If you have a crockpot or slow cooker, it's ideal for this dish.
3 Serve hot, on burger buns, baps, or other soft rolls.

Manicotti

Manicotti is a larger version of canelloni. We have used canelloni for the recipe since it is difficult to find manicotti here. If you find these smaller tubes too fiddly, try using rectangular sheets of lasagne, and rolling them around the filling. Done this way, they most resemble manicotti, and it works just fine. The cheese filling is Kenna's favourite, but you could, of course, use meat.

Serves: 4-6.
10 cannelloni shells or 5 sheets of lasagne cut in half
Topping:
1 tbsp olive oil
1 small onion, chopped
2-3 cloves garlic, crushed
½ small-medium green pepper, chopped
50-85 g/2-3 oz mushrooms, chopped
2 × 150 g/5 oz cans tomato purée with 4 cans of water
a little fresh parsley, chopped
1 tbsp basil
1 tsp black pepper
1 tsp salt
1 tsp oregano
1 tsp sugar
Filling:
225 g/8 oz mozzarella, grated
350 g/12 oz cottage cheese or ricotta
2 eggs
50 g/2 oz grated Parmesan
50 g/2 oz dried breadcrumbs
2 tbsp fresh parsley, chopped
1 tsp sugar
½ tsp salt
½ tsp black pepper

1 Make the sauce: prepare the vegetables and sauté in oil. Add the tomato purée with the water, add the seasonings, and simmer gently for at least an hour – the longer the better. Preheat oven to 180°C/350°F/Gas Mark 4.

2 Cook the pasta as per packet instructions.

3 Meanwhile, make the filling by simply mixing all the ingredients together.

4 When the pasta is cooked, drain well. Fill the canelloni shells. If using lasagne, lay a little of the filling in a line, roll the pasta around it to form a tube, and with a sharp knife, cut the tube free from the rest of the sheet. Repeat until you have used all the filling.

5 Lay the stuffed pasta rolls in an ovenproof dish and cover with the sauce. Sprinkle Parmesan on top and bake for 40-45 minutes.

6 Serve hot with garlic bread and a green side salad.

Note: It is possible – and may even be better – to make this up a day in advance. Just assemble the dish and leave, covered, in the fridge. Heat through when needed.

Overleaf: American pizza
(recipe, page 156)

American pizza

'As most people are probably aware by now, the American pizza is rather different from the traditional Neapolitan variety. Both are delicious. Here is the Yankee version! ,

Serves: about 8-10. For a deep dish-pan, use double the dough.
Dough:
275 g/10 oz plain white flour
1 tsp salt
2 tsp sugar
225 ml/8 fl oz very hot water
3 tsp dried active yeast
25 g/1 oz butter or margarine
Sauce:
1½ tsp olive oil
1½ tsp salad oil
1 small onion, finely diced
2 cloves garlic, crushed
1 × 150 g/5 oz can tomato purée mixed with 300 ml/10 fl oz water
1-2 tsp basil
1-2 tsp oregano
salt and pepper to taste
1 bay leaf
Toppings:
450 g/1 lb cheese (half mozzarella, half Cheddar), grated
275-450 g/10-16 oz Italian salami or pepperoni
1 green pepper, diced
1 onion, chopped
mushrooms
olives

1 In a large bowl, mix the flour, salt and sugar.
2 Into a small bowl, pour the very hot water, add the butter and stir until it has melted. When it has cooled to about blood heat, add the yeast and leave for 5 minutes.
3 Add this mixture to the flour and mix until the dough leaves the side of the bowl – you may have to knead it a little. Form the dough into a ball, transfer to a lightly oiled bowl, cover, and leave in a warm place to rise until it has doubled in size (1-2 hours).
4 Make the sauce: sauté the onion in the oils. Add the garlic and cook until soft. Stir in the tomato purée and water, blending until smooth. Add the seasonings and cook, uncovered, on a low heat for about 1 hour.
5 Prepare the toppings: use all or some of the ingredients listed above, or choose your own.
6 Grease your pan – it is now possible to buy pizza pans, but if you haven't one, use a metal baking tray or tin. Preheat the oven to 230°C/450°F/Gas Mark 8.
7 When the dough has risen, place it on the pan and pat out from the centre until it covers the pan. Make the edges about 5 mm/¼ in thick. (Make sure your fingers are well greased before handling the dough.)
8 Spread the sauce thinly on the pizza. (Extra sauce may be stored in the refrigerator – it will be fine for about 2 weeks.)
9 Spread the sausage slices evenly over the pizza. Add a layer of onions, then peppers and whatever else you're using. The grated cheese is the final topping – cover the pizza generously.
10 Place in the oven and bake for 15-20 minutes – the crust should be brown and the cheese melted.

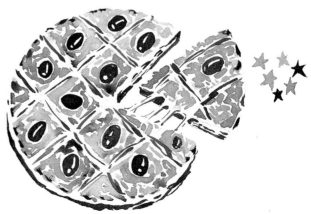

Barbecued beans

❛You could cook the beans from scratch, but here we've used canned – those actually sold as Barbecue beans – or you could use Baked beans. ❜

Serves: 6-8 as a side dish.
2 × 450 g/1 lb cans beans
1 small onion, finely diced
8 tbsp tomato ketchup
1 tbsp mustard (yellow, sold as 'American' is best)
1 tbsp Worcester sauce
1-2 tbsp cider vinegar
85 g/3 oz soft brown sugar or molasses
2 cloves garlic, crushed
2 slices streaky bacon, diced and fried

1 Dice the bacon, and fry it while you mix the other ingredients. Drain the beans of their juice.
2 Mix all ingredients well and place in a casserole or other ovenproof dish. Bake at 150°C/300°F/Gas Mark 2 for 2 hours.
Note: The barbecue sauce is quite sweet. If you don't have a sweet tooth you can reduce or omit the brown sugar.

French-fried onion rings

❛A favourite accompaniment for barbecues, these are also served as a snack food. ❜

Serves: 6 as a side dish.
2 large Spanish onions
oil for deep frying
Batter:
115 g/4 oz flour
½ tsp salt
225 ml/8 fl oz milk
1 egg, beaten

1 Make the batter by mixing all the ingredients and beating well. Let it stand while you prepare the onions.
2 Peel and slice the onions into rings 5-10 mm/¼-½ in thick. Separate the rings. (It is easier to work with large, rather than small onions.)
3 Heat the oil – you need it at least 4 cm/1½ in deep, and really hot. Coat each onion ring in the batter and carefully drop into the fat. Fry until it is a deep golden colour. Don't do too many at a time – they tend to stick together.
4 Remove and place on absorbent paper to drain. If the rings then go soggy, return them to the pan for another minute or two and they will crispen.
5 Serve hot with the dipping sauce of your choice: barbecue sauce (see recipe on page 160) is a family favourite, with sweet and sour sauce a close second. Tomato ketchup is fine, or you may like to try teriyaki or plain soy, but Miranda likes these with mayonnaise!

Potato salad

There are so many recipes for potato salad – this has a slight sweet-sourness which is a bit unusual. It's commonly served with Sloppy Joes, or for any kind of barbecue or party. The recipe below makes a goodly amount!

Serves: 6-8.
2.25 kg/5 lb potatoes (waxy better than floury)
4 eggs, hardboiled, diced
1 bunch spring onions
120 ml/4 fl oz vinaigrette (use bought if you like)
2 large sticks celery, diced
2 pickled gherkins (for authenticity use sweet pickled gherkins)
225 g/8 oz mayonnaise
4 tbsp prepared mustard (what is sold here as 'German' mustard has about the right taste and strength)
3 tsp salt

1 Clean but don't peel the potatoes. Boil them until tender, and drain. Hardboil the eggs. Chop the spring onions.
2 When the potatoes have cooled a little, remove their skins, and cut the potatoes into chunks. Place in a bowl with the spring onions, add the vinaigrette, mix in, and chill for 1 hour.
3 Chop the eggs, celery, and gherkins. Mix the mustard and salt into the mayonnaise.
4 Add the mayonnaise, with the eggs, celery and gherkins to the potatoes. Mix gently – try not to break up the potatoes – and chill for another 2 hours or so.

Marinated three-bean salad

This is a colourful salad with an unusually sweet marinade – good party food. The original recipe calls for wax beans, red kidneys, and green beans, which we also call French beans, or stringless beans. Wax beans are a yellow French bean difficult to find here, so we suggest that you use any other sort of green bean: it is not uncommon for chickpeas (garbanzos) to be used as well.

Serves: 6-8.
1 large can red kidney beans
1 large can French beans or green beans
1 large can other beans – flageolet are good
1 large can chickpeas (optional)
1 large onion, chopped
1 red pepper, chopped (or use canned pimiento, but the fresh pepper adds crunch)
Marinade:
50 ml/2 fl oz light vegetable oil
120 ml/4 fl oz cider vinegar
50 g/2 oz white sugar
1 tsp salt
½ tsp black pepper

1 Chop the vegetables, and place in a serving bowl.
2 Drain the beans well. Chop the green beans into 2.5-4 cm/1-1½ in pieces. Add to the vegetables.
3 Mix the marinade, and pour over the salad. Stir well, and leave, covered, in the refrigerator for up to 2 days – the longer the better. If you find it too sweet, adjust by adding a little more vinegar, and stir it in well.
Note: Actual amounts of beans aren't important – what you need is equal quantities. If you end up using just green beans with the kidneys, for colour's sake you could add some yellow pepper along with the red.

Left: Hamburgers (recipe, page 152), Jello salad (recipe, page 160) and Marinated three-bean salad

Jello salad

'These jellies are very popular all over the United States and there are as many recipes as there are combinations of jelly flavours, fruit, vegetables and relishes. They are served as a salad along with a buffet-style meal, but also crop up as a starter. '

Serves: 8-10 as a side dish: it's usual to serve small portions. Alternatively, makes a useful dessert.
2 × 135 g/4¾ oz pkts of jelly (peach is good, or any red fruit flavour)
225 g/8 oz cream cheese
1 × 400 g/14 oz can fruit cocktail (or any other fruit)

1 Drain the fruit cocktail, reserving the syrup.
2 Make the jelly according to the packet instructions, using the reserved fruit syrup made up to liquid quantity required with cold water.
3 Pour half the jelly mix into a blender goblet. Add the cream cheese and blend until smooth. Pour into a 1.2 l/40 fl oz mould and place in the refrigerator to set for two hours.
4 Pour the other half of the jelly mix into a container, and place in the refrigerator. When partially set, stir in the fruit cocktail, and spoon into the mould on top of the cream cheese jelly. Return to the refrigerator to set for two hours.
5 To serve, unmould onto a plate.

Barbecue sauce

'Here's Kenna's basic recipe – play around until you come up with your own special blend. Very good painted on meat (spare ribs, steaks, chicken, even hamburgers) before grilling. '

Makes: about 600 ml/20 fl oz.
2 small onions, diced
300 ml/10 fl oz tomato ketchup
50 g/2 oz yellow mustard ('American' or 'German')
3 cloves garlic, crushed
2 tbsp Worcester sauce
2 tbsp lemon juice
1 tbsp cider vinegar
1 tbsp soy sauce
1 heaped tsp brown sugar
1 heaped tsp paprika
4 dashes Tabasco sauce

1 Chop the onions finely, and put in the blender goblet with all the other ingredients. Blend until smooth. Taste and adjust if necessary.
2 It is ready for use. Otherwise, store in a screwtop jar, in the refrigerator. It keeps well.

Candied sweet potatoes

Serves: 4.
*2 large sweet potatoes
a little salt
85 ml/3 fl oz water
115 g/4 oz dark brown sugar
25 g/1 oz butter or margarine
4-6 white marshmallows, halved*

❝A vegetable side dish tradition-ally served with the ham or turkey on feast days such as Thanksgiving or Christmas, this rich sweet dish is perhaps something of an acquired taste for most Brits. We include it anyway – go on, be adventurous! ❞

1 Scrub the sweet potatoes, and place whole in a pan of cold water. Bring to the boil. Cook until tender (about 30 minutes). Drain and cool a little.
2 Peel, and chop the potatoes into largish chunks, and sprinkle with salt.
3 In a thick-bottomed saucepan or frying pan, put the water, sugar, and butter/margarine, and, stirring, bring to boil.
4 Add the sweet potato chunks, turning often so that they are coated in the syrup, and have a glazed look.
5 Just before the potatoes are ready (after about 10 minutes), add the marshmallows, allowing them to melt a little.
6 Serve hot.

Traditional New England cranberry relish

Makes: about 600 ml/20 fl oz.
*225-275 g/8-10 oz fresh cranberries
1 small onion
150 ml/5 fl oz sour cream
115 g/4 oz white sugar
2 tbsp horseradish relish*

❝Quite the best recipe we have discovered – our thanks to Tjaki Heidema from Maine, who sent it to us. The cranberries really need to be fresh – they are difficult, but not impossible to find. ❞

1 Mince together the cranberries and the onion.
2 Beat together the sour cream, sugar and horseradish relish. Stir in the minced berry mixture. Turn into an airtight container and freeze for at least 24 hours.
3 A few hours before you wish to serve, retrieve from the freezer. Allow to thaw, and then whip the mixture. Serve as an accompaniment to meat.
Serving suggestions: This is usually served with the Thanksgiving turkey or ham, but it is also excellent with rabbit.

Oyster dressing

> ❛To make this dressing you first need to make some cornbread, which is a simple process – see our recipe on page 145. ❜

For a 5.5-7 kg/12-16 lb turkey.
350 g/12 oz cornbread (stale), crumbled
115 g/4 oz butter or margarine
1 medium onion, finely chopped
225 g/8 oz dried breadcrumbs
1 egg, beaten
1-2 sticks celery, finely chopped
1 tsp salt
1 tsp black pepper
1 tsp sage
225 g/8 oz oysters, canned or fresh
225 ml/8 fl oz milk
50-120 ml/2-4 oz stock or clear consommé (optional – for a moister dressing)

1 If you haven't any in hand, make up the cornbread a couple of days beforehand.
2 Melt the butter/margarine in a frying pan, add the onion, and sauté until soft. Stir in about half the dried breadcrumbs. Remove from the heat and pour this mixture into a large mixing bowl.
3 If you are using fresh oysters, shuck them (see page 13, steps 3 and 4).
4 Add all the remaining ingredients, holding back with the stock until you can judge what consistency you require. (You may not need any of it.)
5 Stuff the mixture into the turkey, and bake.

Traditional sausage dressing

> ❛This tasty stuffing will appeal to the more conventional, who may shun the Oyster dressing above. ❜

For a 5.5-7 kg/12-16 lb turkey.
450 g/1 lb pork sausage meat
1 medium onion, chopped
1-2 sticks celery, chopped
115 g/4 oz butter
450 g/1 lb seasoned stuffing mix (use your preferred packet mix)
450 ml/15 fl oz chicken stock or 1 stock cube in equal amount of water
2 eggs, beaten

1 Cook the sausage meat until it is no longer pink. Pour off the grease.
2 Prepare the vegetables and add to the sausage meat, with the butter. Cook gently until the vegetables are tender.
3 Empty the stuffing mix into a large bowl and add the chicken stock. Stir in the sausage meat mixture and then the beaten eggs. Mix well and stuff into the turkey.

Right: Thanksgiving dinner with Traditional New England cranberry relish (recipe, page 161)

Angel food cake

about 150 g/5 oz plain white flour (but see 2 below)
250 g/9 oz caster sugar
1 tsp salt
10-12 egg whites (must be at room temperature – don't use straight from the refrigerator)
1 tbsp water
1 tbsp lemon juice
1 tsp cream of tartar
½ tsp vanilla essence
½ tsp almond essence

❝Oh, this is indeed heavenly – light as a feather, too light even to cut with a knife. Its flavour is gently almond, the texture fluffy and melt-in-the-mouth. Often used as a base for fruit flans, it's also very good with fruit purées or syrups, but just as often served with a light glaze or sugar icing.

In this recipe it's volume rather than weight that matters, so it's difficult to be exact about all the measures. ❞

1 Preheat the oven to 180°C/350°F/Gas Mark 4. Have ready your 23 cm/9 in pan or ring mould, thoroughly clean and grease-free – the smallest amount will prevent the cake from rising properly. (In the States, there are special pans for Angel food cake, which you just might find here.)
2 Sift the flour into a measuring jug until you have it up to the 225 ml/8 fl oz mark – this will give you the right volume.
3 Sift the sugar. Now set aside 175 g/6 oz and resift the remaining 85 g/3 oz with the flour, and the salt. Repeat this procedure three times. (Don't be tempted to skip these siftings – it needs as much air as it can get.)
4 Add the water and lemon juice to the egg whites (use 10-12 according to size), and whisk until foamy. Add the cream of tartar and whisk until stiff. Now sprinkle in the sugar, 1 tablespoon at a time, and beat in. Add the vanilla and almond, and whisk until thick and glossy.
5 Gently fold in the sugar-flour mixture, sprinkling it 2 tablespoons at a time on to the egg whites. Turn into the pan and bake for 45 minutes.
6 When the cake is done – the top will be golden brown – remove from the oven and invert the tin over a funnel, or other likely object. This is to allow air to circulate underneath the tin. Failing that, prop the tin, upside down, on cans spaced evenly around the circle. Leave to cool for 1½ hours. Then gently free the cake with a palette knife and turn out on to a plate. Don't cut the cake with a knife – the texture is such that it will revert to a doughy paste. In America they have cake dividers of metal with widely spaced prongs, which somewhat resemble Afro combs. Don't worry if you haven't the right tool – break the cake with a long-pronged fork, and gently pull apart. The cake will keep well: wrap in foil (only when completely cooled) and store in the fridge.

Chocolate cheesecake

Biscuit crust:
225-275 g/8-10 oz digestive (or chocolate-flavoured) biscuits, crushed
about 115 g/4 oz butter or margarine, melted
Filling:
350 g/12 oz plain chocolate chips or block
450 g/1 lb cream cheese, softened
450 g/1 lb granulated or caster sugar
4 eggs
3 tsp cocoa
2 tsp vanilla essence
300 ml/10 fl oz sour cream (or plain yoghurt)

❝This is a dense, moist, rich and heavy cheesecake – a world away from those light creamy varieties. What more to say: it's utterly delicious – every chocolate-lover's dream! ❞

1 Make the biscuit crust: crush the biscuits, add the melted butter/margarine, mix well, and pat into a 25 cm/10 in fairly deep spring-form or very large flan tin to form the base and sides of a shell. Chill.
2 In a double boiler, over hot, but not boiling water, set the chocolate to melt. If using block chocolate, break it up first.
3 Soften the cream cheese and beat with the sugar. Add the eggs, one at a time, and mix well.
4 Add the cocoa and the vanilla to the cheese mixture. Beat in the melted chocolate, mix thoroughly and stir in the sour cream/yoghurt.
5 When it is well blended, pour into the biscuit crust and chill for several hours before serving.

Strawberry cake

225 g/8 oz fresh strawberries, crushed
1 × 135 g/4¾ oz pkt strawberry jelly
120 ml/4 fl oz boiling water
1 × 450 g/1 lb sponge mix
4 eggs
120 ml/4 fl oz vegetable oil
Icing:
250 g/9 oz icing sugar
115 g/4 oz margarine, softened
a few strawberries

6 'Pudding' cakes – put together with things in packets that make up instant puddings – are very popular in America, and we make no apology for including one here. This cake calls for a packet of jelly, and is quick to make to round off a summer meal. It's much the best with fresh strawberries, but frozen will do – canned, although they may be used, really aren't too nice. **9**

1 Preheat the oven to 180°C/350°F/Gas Mark 4. Lightly grease a 23 cm/9 in ring mould.
2 Prepare the strawberries, reserving as much of the juice as possible.
3 Melt the jelly in boiling water.
4 Put the sponge mix in a large mixing bowl. Add the crushed strawberries, and their juice, the eggs and the oil, and stir in the melted jelly. Mix together well and pour into the cake tin.
5 Bake for 40-45 minutes. When the cake has cooled a little, turn out, but leave to cool completely before icing.
6 Make the icing: cream the icing sugar and the margarine. Add enough strawberries, crushing them, to make the mixture creamy in consistency.
7 Ice the cake, and decorate with a few whole or halved strawberries.

Crème de menthe brownies

Brownie layer:
225 g/8 oz white sugar
115 g/4 oz butter or margarine
4 eggs, beaten
115 g/4 oz plain white flour
½ tsp salt
475 ml/16 fl oz chocolate syrup
1 tsp vanilla essence
50 g/2 oz nuts, chopped
Crème de menthe icing:
115 g/4 oz butter or margarine
250 g/9 oz icing sugar
2 tbsp crème de menthe
a little milk
Chocolate glaze:
175 g/6 oz plain chocolate, chips or block
85 g/3 oz butter or margarine

6 There must be dozens of Brownie recipes – many variations on the chocolate theme, others marbled with cream cheese, or 'blonde' versions, made with brown sugar. To achieve the perfect moist richness of these brownies you really need to use chocolate syrup instead of solid chocolate – it is now available in some stores. **9**

1 Preheat the oven to 180°C/350°F/Gas Mark 4. Grease a 23 × 33 cm/9 × 13 in pan. Mix all the brownie ingredients together and pour into the greased tin. Bake for 30 minutes. Remove from oven but leave in the pan. Cool a little before icing.
2 Make the icing: cream the margarine with the sugar and the crème de menthe. Add a little milk (1-2 tablespoons should be enough) to get a spreading consistency. Spread on the brownie layer and cool well before glazing.
3 Make the chocolate glaze: melt the chocolate with the butter/margarine, stirring gently. Spread over the mint layer. Smooth the surface and chill overnight. Brownies are often just cut into squares and served from the tin.

Overleaf: Chocolate cheesecake (recipe, page 164), Angel food cake, Rocky road clusters and Oatmeal drop cookies (recipes, page 169)

*Right: A selection of cocktails
(recipes, pages 170-1)*

Muffins

'American muffins are like neither the traditional English muffins (of dim memory, alas), nor what are sold packaged as 'English-style' muffins. Since Americans often bake them in little paper cake cases, they look like fairy cakes but in texture are far more like the drop scone or griddle cake. Possibly the most well-known variety is the blueberry muffin – blueberries are rather hard to come by here so we've tried two substitutes: elderberries and blackcurrants. The blackcurrants are closer in taste to the US blueberries; elderberries are sharper, but make a nice change. '

Makes: about 24. Or bake the dough in a loaf tin.
175-225 g/6-8 oz berries (you can use canned blackcurrants)
225 g/8 oz plain white flour
50-115 g/2-4 oz sugar, caster or granulated (amount depends on choice of berries)
½ tsp salt
2 tsp baking powder
2 eggs
50 g/2 oz butter or margarine
4-5 tbsp milk
½ tsp lemon rind (optional – we think it greatly improves the taste)
24 paper cake cases, laid on a baking sheet or in pie tins

1 Preheat the oven to 200°C/400°F/Gas Mark 6. Prepare the berries: if using elderberries or fresh blackcurrants, they should be rinsed and well drained, and dried off as much as possible; if using canned berries, drain as much as possible, and gently roll in a little flour before adding to the batter. (A can of blackberries yields about half the stated weight of fruit when drained.)
2 Sift together into a large mixing bowl the flour, sugar, salt, and baking powder. If using elderberries, use about 115 g/4 oz sugar – for blackcurrants, 50 g/2 oz.
3 Set the butter/margarine to melt on very gentle heat. Beat the eggs and add to the dry ingredients.
4 Add the milk to the melted butter/margarine and pour into the flour and egg mixture. Add the lemon rind, mixing all lightly together. Don't overbeat or the dough can toughen: the consistency should be dropping, not pouring.
5 Gently fold in the berries. Spoon the batter into the paper cases – about I dessertspoon in each. Bake for about 15 minutes (longer if baking a loaf). They can look pretty pallid, but if you touch the top with your finger and it doesn't 'give', they are done. They should be fairly moist inside, but we don't mean runny and uncooked! Remove and cool slightly.
6 Best served warm, with or without butter. We rather liked them with cream cheese, too. They may be reheated – just wrap in foil and pop into the oven for a few minutes.

Banana bread

'A delicious sweet (but not too sweet) bread. We've suggested using three bananas, but if you like it really heavy, add a couple more. '

115 g/4 oz butter or margarine
225 g/8 oz granulated sugar
2 eggs, beaten
I tsp lemon juice
3 medium bananas, mashed (soft and ripe, but not black)
225 g/8 oz plain white flour
3 tsps baking powder
½ tsp salt
50-85 g/2-3 oz nuts, chopped (preferably walnuts)

1 Preheat the oven to 160°C/325°F/Gas Mark 3. Grease a 900 g/2 lb loaf tin.
2 Cream the fat and sugar, and when well blended, mix in the beaten eggs.
3 Mash the bananas and stir in the lemon juice. Add to the creamed mixture.
4 Stir in the flour, and the baking powder and salt. When thoroughly mixed, add the nuts, and turn out into the tin. Bake in the centre of the oven for about I hour and 15 minutes.
5 Turn out and cool on a rack before serving. It can be eaten with butter, or just as it comes.

Oatmeal drop cookies

Sweet crunchy mouthfuls of candy.

Makes: about 40.
150 ml/5 fl oz milk
450 g/1 lb white sugar
1 tbsp butter or margarine
pinch of salt
1 tsp vanilla essence
175 g/6 oz crunchy peanut butter
200 g/7 oz oatflakes (we use porridge oats)

1 Grease a large baking sheet.
2 Put the milk, sugar, butter/margarine, salt, and vanilla essence into a saucepan and bring slowly to the boil, stirring. Boil for 2 minutes.
3 Remove from the heat, stir in the peanut butter, and add the oatflakes. Mix well.
4 Drop heaped teaspoons of the mixture on to the baking sheet, and leave to set. They will be hardening already, so don't hang about!

Rocky road clusters

Rocky road candies, cookies, and ice cream (chocolate ice cream with nuts, raisins, and marshmallows) are part of the landscape for American children of all ages – and they've just recently marketed a Rocky road breakfast cereal too!

Makes: 40-50.
16 white marshmallows
175 g/6 oz walnuts or pecan nuts, coarsely chopped
150-175 g/5-6 oz raisins or sultanas
450 g/1 lb plain chocolate
knob of butter

1 Grease two baking sheets.
2 Cut the marshmallows into small pieces – quarters or even eighths. Chop the nuts, and weigh out the raisins/sultanas.
3 Melt the chocolate gently in the top of a double boiler or in a bowl over hot, but not boiling water. Add a little knob of butter to aid the process.
4 When the chocolate has thoroughly melted, remove from the heat, mix in the marshmallows, nuts and raisins, so they are all well coated. Drop tablespoons of the mixture onto the baking sheets. Leave to cool and set hard.
Note: Don't skimp on the chocolate – if you haven't the full amount cut back on the other ingredients, or you'll find it just won't mix well.

Foolproof fudge

More properly known as Chocolate marshmallow fudge, we retitled it simply because it is the only recipe we have ever discovered which always turns out well. The only problem is getting it into the dish before it sets! It is very smooth and extremely rich – we think it probably keeps well but to be honest we've never been allowed to put that to the test!

Makes: about 900 g/2 lb.
550 g/1¼ lb granulated sugar
250 g/9 oz marshmallows
50 g/2 oz butter or margarine
175 ml/6 fl oz evaporated milk
1 tsp vanilla essence
350 g/12 oz plain chocolate (chips, or block, broken into pieces)
50 g/2 oz chopped nuts (optional)
50-115 g/2-4 oz raisins (optional)

1 Lightly grease a fairly shallow pan or dish (we use a Swiss roll tin). The dish should be at least 2.5 in/1 in deep.
2 In a heavy-bottomed pan, combine the sugar, marshmallows, butter/margarine and milk, and stirring, cook over a medium heat until it boils. Reduce the heat to low, and let it boil gently, stirring all the while, for 5 minutes.
3 Remove from the heat, add the vanilla and the chocolate pieces and keep stirring until the chocolate melts and is thoroughly mixed in. If you want to add any nuts and raisins mix them in quickly now, and turn out the rapidly setting mixture into the pan. Leave to cool thoroughly before cutting into squares.

Drinks

Sazerac

A true Bayou cocktail.

Makes: I cocktail
65 ml/2½ fl oz bourbon or rye
4 tsp caster sugar
¼ tsp Angostura bitters
3-4 ice cubes
3 dashes Pernod
lemon twist

1 Chill a glass. In a bowl or jug, mix the bourbon/rye with the sugar, the bitters, and the ice cubes, stirring until the sugar dissolves.
2 Pour the Pernod into the chilled glass and tip from side to side, swirling until the glass is coated. Pour out the remainder.
3 Place a strainer over the glass and pour in the bourbon or rye mix. Serve with a twist of lemon.

Ramos fizz

An excellent drink for brunches!

Makes: I drink.
40 ml/1½ fl oz gin
I egg
I tsp icing sugar
juice of half a lemon
juice of half a lime
25 ml/1 fl oz single cream
3 dashes orange-flower water
crushed ice

1 Crush the ice, and place it in a glass. Put all the other ingredients into a blender goblet, and whizz for a few seconds.
2 Pour into the glass over the crushed ice.

Margarita

This is a must with a Tex-Mex meal. In restaurants it's served by the pitcher!

Makes: I drink
I measure Tequila
I measure Triple Sec or other orange liqueur
1½ measures lime cordial
½ measure lemon juice (bottled, rather than fresh)
salt to coat glass

1 Rub a little lemon juice around the rim of a glass, and then dip it in salt to coat.
2 Mix the ingredients in a blender or shaker, and pour into the glass over crushed ice.

Pina colada

A Tex-Mex special.

Makes: 2 drinks
50 g/2 oz creamed coconut, mixed to paste with a little water
I tbsp icing sugar
225 ml/8 fl oz unsweetened pineapple juice
85 ml/3 fl oz white rum

1 Make a coconut paste, as packet directions, with water or use Coco Lopez canned creamed coconut (without adding water).
2 Blend the coconut paste with all other ingredients and pour into a glass over crushed ice. If liked, garnish with a cherry on a stick, or a piece of pineapple.

Smuggler

A real winter warmer, much favoured by skiers.

Makes: I mugful.
drinking chocolate or cocoa, to taste
about 300 ml/10 fl oz milk
I measure peppermint Schnapps
whipped cream

1 Warm the milk and make up cocoa/chocolate to taste.
2 Add the Schnapps, and top with a dollop of whipped cream.

Mai tai

The Hawaiian drink!

Makes: I drink.
25 ml/1 fl oz white rum
25 ml/1 fl oz black rum
I tbsp Cointreau or other orange liqueur
15 ml/½ fl oz lime juice
85 ml/3 fl oz pineapple juice

1 Mix ingredients together and pour over cracked ice.
2 Garnish with a stick of pineapple and a maraschino cherry.

Planters' punch

An exotic island blend.

Makes: I drink.
85 ml/3 fl oz black rum
juice of ½ lemon
juice of ½ orange
4 dashes Curacao

1 Mix ingredients and pour into a tall glass over cracked ice.
2 Garnish with a cherry, pineapple, and half-slices of lemon and orange.

Singapore sling

True to its name, this has travelled from Singapore, and is much enjoyed in the Hawaiian islands.

Makes: 1 drink.
50 ml/2 fl oz gin
50 ml/2 fl oz cherry brandy
juice of ½ lemon
1 tsp icing sugar

1 Shake ingredients together, with ice, and pour into a tall glass.
2 Garnish with a stick of pineapple, an orange slice and a maraschino cherry.

Milwaukee-style grasshopper

Grasshoppers (so called because of their colour) are usually served as after-dinner drinks.

Serves: 3-4.
50 ml/2 fl oz crème de cacao
50 ml/2 fl oz crème de menthe
½ l/18 fl oz pack vanilla ice cream or 50 ml/2 fl oz cream

1 Have everything ready and to hand: work quickly – you don't want the ice cream to melt too much.
2 Put all the ingredients into a blender goblet, and give them a quick whizz. Pour into champagne or sherbet glasses, and serve immediately.

Long island tea

Long Island tea tastes exactly like traditional iced tea, but don't try to drive a car after even one!

Makes: 1 drink.
1 part white rum
1 part tequila
1 part vodka
1 part gin
1 Coca-cola
1 part Sweet & Sour Mix or substitute a mixture of 1½ measures lime cordial to ½ measure lemon juice

1 Mix all ingredients together in a tall glass, with ice.
2 Decorate with a slice of lemon.

Manhattan

This famous American drink is well worth trying.

Makes: 1 drink.
1 part sweet vermouth
3 parts bourbon
dash of angostura bitters

1 Stir all ingredients together with cracked ice.
2 Strain and serve in a cocktail glass, decorated with a cherry.

Hot buttered rum

This one will thaw every inch of you, right to your frozen toes! Apparently, it was a favourite with the Pilgrim Fathers – for purely medicinal purposes, no doubt!

Makes: 1 drink, served in a large mug.
50 ml/2 fl oz white or black rum
1 stick of cinnamon about 10 cm/4 in long (or as long as the mug is tall)
2-4 whole cloves
1 tsp sugar
boiling water
knob of butter

1 Pour the rum into the mug and add the cinnamon stick, cloves and the sugar.
2 Fill up the mug with boiling water and float a knob of butter on top. Give it a quick stir and drink while it's hot – the rum sipped through the melting butter is sensational, but congealed globules of fat in a cold liquid are too awful to contemplate, let alone drink!

Mint julep

As much a tradition at the Kentucky Derby as are strawberries and cream at Wimbledon, whether you are actually there or watching it on television.

Makes: 1 drink.
2 shots bourbon
1 tsp icing sugar
sprig of fresh mint
soda water

1 In a glass, jug, or bowl, crush the mint with the sugar. Add a splash of soda, mash again, and add the bourbon.
2 Pour through a strainer into a tall glass filled with crushed ice. Stir until the glass frosts (or put in the refrigerator). Decorate with sprigs of mint.

Glossary

US terms	UK terms for nearest equivalents
Biscuits	Scones.
Butter	Unless specified, use salted butter.
Butter, sweet	Unsalted butter.
Cheese, Monterey Jack	Use Mozzarella, or half-and-half mozzarella and mild Cheddar.
Cheese, Swiss	Emmenthal or Gruyere.
Chilli powder	Use McCormick's Chilli Seasoning – US chilli powder is not just cayenne, but has added spices.
Chips	Potato crisps.
Chocolate, plain, unsweetened	Very bitter cooking chocolate. 'Plain' is also a term used to describe any dessert chcolate without such things as nuts in it.
Chocolate, semi-sweet	Plain: Menier, Bournville, etc.
Chocolate, sweet	Milk chocolate.
Chocolate, sprinkles	Chocolate vermicelli.
Club soda	Soda water.
Cookies	Sweet biscuits.
Cookies, Oreo	A brand similar to custard creams, but chocolate-flavoured biscuit with vanilla cream filling – use Bourbon creams.
Cornstarch	Cornflour. Use arrowroot if the mixture is to become clear.
Cracked wheat	Bulghar (Burghal) wheat, cous-cous, pourgourri.
Crackers	Cheese biscuits.
Crackers, Graham	Use digestive biscuits.
Crackers, soda	Use plain cream crackers.
Cream, light, coffee	Single cream.
Cream, heavy	Double cream.
Dream Whip	Brand name for dried cream powder, which, reconstituted and whipped, becomes whipped cream.
Dollar pancakes	Rather small versions of Scotch pancakes/griddle scones.
Flapjacks	Pancakes
Flour, all-purpose	Plain white flour. If for bread, use strong white.
Flour, cake	Refined white flour.
Flour, Graham, wholewheat	Wholemeal (UK wholewheat flour is different from both US whole-wheat and UK wholemeal, being a mixture of wholemeal and white).
French fries	Chips.
French toast	Not the thin, curly, crisp toast, but bread dipped in egg, fried in butter, and eaten for breakfast, with syrup, icing sugar, or marmalade.
Jello	Jelly, as in dessert.
Jelly	Jelly as in seedless jam.
Karo, corn syrup	Corn syrup is now available in some supermarkets here but it is expensive. In cooking, use half golden syrup, half molasses.
Lady fingers	Boudoir fingers, sponge fingers.
Meat Rib-eye, Sirloin, T-bone, Filet Mignon	Use tenderest cuts of steak.
Round steak, stew meat, chop meat, ground beef	Use braising, stewing steak.
Hamburger meat	Use beef mince.
Commercially packed bacon	Use streaky bacon.
Pickle meat	Use gammon.
Salt pork	Use green (unsmoked) bacon.
Cornish hen	We don't have these small fowl – use squab pigeon.
Miracle Whip	Brand name for a somewhat vinegary, seasoned mayonnaise-type dressing; consistency of mayonnaise, tastes like salad cream.
Muffins, American	Like a rather doughy cake, eaten for breakfast.
Muffins, 'English-style'	More like a bread roll, available now in UK supermarkets.
Oatmeal	Oatflakes.
Nuts Filberts	Hazelnuts.
Macadamia	Now available in large supermarkets. Brazils are close in texture; taste is a cross between brazil and cashew.
Pulses Black-eye peas	Black-eyed beans.
Garbanzos	Chickpeas.
Saltines (soda crackers)	Use water biscuits, but if using in cooking, add salt.
Seafood Crawfish, Crayfish	Use Dublin Bay prawns. In the US they tend not to differentiate.
Shrimps	Use prawns (in the US 'shrimp' is used rather as a generic term – anyway, our shrimps are too small).

Shortening, Crisco	Use solid vegetable oil, (*not* lard).
Spaghetti squash	Vegetable spaghetti.
Sugar	If unspecified, use granulated.
Sugar, light brown	Soft brown.
Sugar, dark brown	Muscovado, or molasses. There is no equivalent to demerara sugar.
Sugar, confectioners, XX	Icing sugar.
Sugar, powdered, superfine	Caster.
Tomato paste	Tomato purée, concentrate.
Tomato purée	More like passata.
Tomato sauce	Not a ketchup, but a thinner blend of puréed fruit and juice.
Vanilla extract	Vanilla essence.

Vegetables	
Beans, fava	Use broad beans.
Beans, lima	Sometimes available, tinned, but if not use broad beans.
Beans, string	Runner beans.
Beets	Beetroot.
Celery knob/root	Celeriac.
Chicory	Endive.
Corn	Sweetcorn, maize (*not* wheat).
Eggplant	Aubergine.
Endive	Chicory.
Lettuce, head	If unspecified, use iceberg.
Romaine	Cos lettuce.
Peppers, bell, sweet	Capsicums, green peppers.
Pimento	Red peppers.
Rutabaga	Swede.
Scallions	Spring onions.
Squash	Generic term for gourd/marrow family, with many varieties.
Squash, spaghetti	Vegetable spaghetti.
Squash, summer	Yellow crookneck courgettes.
Zucchini	Courgette.

Cooking Terms

Coffee cake	Cake to be eaten with coffee (not coffee-flavoured).
Dessert	Pudding.
Pudding	Refers only to set custard-type desserts, like blancmange, vanilla mould.
Sherbet	Sorbet, granita (water-ice).
Angel Food pan, Bundt pan	Use a ring mould.
Broiler	Grill.
Kettle	Saucepan, usually large soup pan.
Saran wrap, Clear wrap	Clingfilm.

Equivalent measures US/metric/Imperial

You may find it useful to know that a US measuring cup is approximately the size of the 225 g/8 oz cottage cheese carton. You could calibrate the plastic carton with a waterproof marker pen: place the full carton on the kitchen scales, weigh out 50 g/2 oz of the cheese, level off the remainder, and mark. This would give you the ¾-cup level. Repeat and you will have the ½-cup mark. Repeat again, and mark ¼-cup. This is pretty rough and ready, but will do for most things!

Now for the thing most baffling to the British – here's how to measure ¼-cup of butter. Fill the cup (or cottage cheese carton) to ¼-cup mark, with water. Add butter until the water is level with the ½-cup mark. Pour off the water – the butter you have left is ¼-cup! Simple, once you know how!

Food	Cup	Metric	Imperial
Butter/margarine	1	225 g	8 oz
1 stick of butter	½	50 g	4 oz
Bananas, mashed	1	225 g	8 oz
Cheese, cottage	1	225 g	8 oz
grated	1	95 g	3¼ oz
Chocolate	1 square	25 g	1 oz
Cocoa	1	115 g	4 oz
Flour, all-purpose	1	115 g	4 oz
Milk	1	225 ml	8 fl oz
Potatoes, mashed	1	225 g	8 oz raw, unpeeled
Raisins	1	175 g	6 oz
Rice, long grain, uncooked	1	175 g	6 oz
Sugar, granulated	1	225 g	8 oz
brown (packed down)	1	175 g	6 oz
icing (confectioners)	1	125 g	4½ oz
Macaroni (dry)	1	115 g	4 oz
Oil	1	225 ml	8 fl oz

Liquid measurements

NB: It is important to remember, when using American recipes, that the US pint = 16 fl oz = 475 ml, while the Imperial pint = 20 fl oz = 600 ml. You may also find fluids measured in tablespoons.

475 ml = 16 fl oz = 32 tbsp = 2 cups = 1 US pint
225 ml = 8 fl oz = 16 tbsp = 1 cup = ½ US pint
120 ml = 4 fl oz = 8 tbsp = ½ cup = ¼ US pint
 50 ml = 2 fl oz = 4 tbsp = ¼ cup = 1 large jigger
 35 ml = 1½ fl oz = 3 tbsp = 1 jigger
 20 ml = 1 fl oz = 2 tbsp = 1 pony
 15 ml = ½ fl oz = 1 tbsp = 3 tsp

Larger quantities you may come across (particularly in drinks recipes):
Split = 6.4 fl oz
Tenth = 12.8 fl oz
Fifth = 25.6 fl oz
Quart = 32 fl oz

The US tablespoon is 15 ml, and the teaspoon, 5 ml. This is the same as the metric spoons now widely used here. Despite the rules about never mixing imperial and metric measurements, we have used the US/metric tablespoon and teaspoon.

Index